Essential
Understanding
Series

Developing
Essential Understanding
of
Proof and Proving
for Teaching Mathematics *in*
Grades 9–12

Amy B. Ellis
University of Wisconsin–Madison
Madison, Wisconsin

Kristen Bieda
Michigan State University
East Lansing, Michigan

Rose Mary Zbiek
Series Editor
The Pennsylvania State University
University Park, Pennsylvania

Eric Knuth
University of Wisconsin–Madison
Madison, Wisconsin

NATIONAL COUNCIL OF
TEACHERS OF MATHEMATICS

Library of Congress Cataloging-in-Publication Data

Ellis, Amy B., author.
   Developing essential understanding of proof and proving for teaching
mathematics in grades 9-12 /Amy B. Ellis, University of Wisconsin-Madison,
Madison, Wisconsin, Kristen Bieda, Michigan State University, East Lansing,
Michigan, Eric Knuth, University of Wisconsin-Madison, Madison, Wisconsin;
Rose Mary Zbiek, series editor, The Pennsylvania State University, University
Park, Pennsylvania.
      pages cm
   Includes bibliographical references.
   ISBN 978-0-87353-675-2
   1. Mathematics--Study and teaching (Secondary) 2. Effective teaching.
I. Bieda, Kristen, author. II. Knuth, Eric J., author. III. Title.
   QA11.2.E55 2012
   510.71'2--dc23
                          2012022242

The National Council of Teachers of Mathematics is a public voice of mathematics education,
supporting teachers to ensure equitable mathematics learning of the highest quality for all
students through vision, leadership, professional development, and research.

Printed in the United States of America

Contents

Foreword

Teaching mathematics in prekindergarten–grade 12 requires a special understanding of mathematics. Effective teachers of mathematics think about and beyond the content that they teach, seeking explanations and making connections to other topics, both inside and outside mathematics. Students meet curriculum and achievement expectations when they work with teachers who know what mathematics is important for each topic that they teach.

The National Council of Teachers of Mathematics (NCTM) presents the Essential Understanding Series in tandem with a call to focus the school mathematics curriculum in the spirit of *Curriculum Focal Points for Prekindergarten through Grade 8 Mathematics: A Quest for Coherence*, published in 2006, and *Focus in High School Mathematics: Reasoning and Sense Making*, released in 2009. The Essential Understanding books are a resource for individual teachers and groups of colleagues interested in engaging in mathematical thinking to enrich and extend their own knowledge of particular mathematics topics in ways that benefit their work with students. The topic of each book is an area of mathematics that is difficult for students to learn, challenging to teach, and critical for students' success as learners and in their future lives and careers.

Drawing on their experiences as teachers, researchers, and mathematicians, the authors have identified the big ideas that are at the heart of each book's topic. A set of essential understandings— mathematical points that capture the essence of the topic—fleshes out each big idea. Taken collectively, the big ideas and essential understandings give a view of a mathematics that is focused, connected, and useful to teachers. Links to topics that students encounter earlier and later in school mathematics and to instruction and assessment practices illustrate the relevance and importance of a teacher's essential understanding of mathematics.

On behalf of the Board of Directors, I offer sincere thanks and appreciation to everyone who has helped to make this series possible. I extend special thanks to Rose Mary Zbiek for her leadership as series editor. I join the Essential Understanding project team in welcoming you to these books and in wishing you many years of continued enjoyment of learning and teaching mathematics.

Henry Kepner
President, 2008–2010
National Council of Teachers of Mathematics

Preface

From prekindergarten through grade 12, the school mathematics curriculum includes important topics that are pivotal in students' development. Students who understand these ideas cross smoothly into new mathematical terrain and continue moving forward with assurance.

However, many of these topics have traditionally been challenging to teach as well as learn, and they often prove to be barriers rather than gateways to students' progress. Students who fail to get a solid grounding in them frequently lose momentum and struggle in subsequent work in mathematics and related disciplines.

The Essential Understanding Series identifies such topics at all levels. Teachers who engage students in these topics play critical roles in students' mathematical achievement. Each volume in the series invites teachers who aim to be not just proficient but outstanding in the classroom—teachers like you—to enrich their understanding of one or more of these topics to ensure students' continued development in mathematics.

How much do you need to know?

To teach these challenging topics effectively, you must draw on a mathematical understanding that is both broad and deep. The challenge is to know considerably more about the topic than you expect your students to know and learn.

Why does your knowledge need to be so extensive? Why must it go above and beyond what you need to teach and your students need to learn? The answer to this question has many parts.

To plan successful learning experiences, you need to understand different models and representations and, in some cases, emerging technologies as you evaluate curriculum materials and create lessons. As you choose and implement learning tasks, you need to know what to emphasize and why those ideas are mathematically important.

While engaging your students in lessons, you must anticipate their perplexities, help them avoid known pitfalls, and recognize and dispel misconceptions. You need to capitalize on unexpected classroom opportunities to make connections among mathematical ideas. If assessment shows that students have not understood the material adequately, you need to know how to address weaknesses that you have identified in their understanding. Your understanding must be sufficiently versatile to allow you to represent the mathematics in different ways to students who don't understand it the first time. In addition, you need to know where the topic fits in the full span of the mathematics curriculum. You must understand where your students are coming from in their thinking and where they are heading mathematically in the months and years to come.

Accomplishing these tasks in mathematically sound ways is a tall order. A rich understanding of the mathematics supports the varied work of teaching as you guide your students and keep their learning on track.

How can the Essential Understanding Series help?

The Essential Understanding books offer you an opportunity to delve into the mathematics that you teach and reinforce your content knowledge. They do not include materials for you to use directly with your students, nor do they discuss classroom management, teaching styles, or assessment techniques. Instead, these books focus squarely on issues of mathematical content—the ideas and understanding that you must bring to your preparation, in-class instruction, one-on-one interactions with students, and assessment.

How do the authors approach the topics?

For each topic, the authors identify "big ideas" and "essential understandings." The big ideas are mathematical statements of overarching concepts that are central to a mathematical topic and link numerous smaller mathematical ideas into coherent wholes. The books call the smaller, more concrete ideas that are associated with each big idea *essential understandings*. They capture aspects of the corresponding big idea and provide evidence of its richness.

The big ideas have tremendous value in mathematics. You can gain an appreciation of the power and worth of these densely packed statements through persistent work with the interrelated essential understandings. Grasping these multiple smaller concepts and through them gaining access to the big ideas can greatly increase your intellectual assets and classroom possibilities.

In your work with mathematical ideas in your role as a teacher, you have probably observed that the essential understandings are often at the heart of the understanding that you need for presenting one of these challenging topics to students. Knowing these ideas very well is critical because they are the mathematical pieces that connect to form each big idea.

Big ideas and essential understandings are identified by icons in the books.

marks a big idea, and

marks an essential understanding.

How are the books organized?

Every book in the Essential Understanding Series has the same structure:

- The introduction gives an overview, explaining the reasons for the selection of the particular topic and highlighting some of the differences between what teachers and students need to know about it.

- Chapter 1 is the heart of the book, identifying and examining the big ideas and related essential understandings.

- Chapter 2 reconsiders the ideas discussed in chapter 1 in light of their connections with mathematical ideas within the grade band and with other mathematics that the students have encountered earlier or will encounter later in their study of mathematics.

- Chapter 3 wraps up the discussion by considering the challenges that students often face in grasping the necessary concepts related to the topic under discussion. It analyzes the development of their thinking and offers guidance for presenting ideas to them and assessing their understanding.

The discussion of big ideas and essential understandings in chapter 1 is interspersed with questions labeled "Reflect." It is important to pause in your reading to think about these on your own or discuss them with your colleagues. By engaging with the material in this way, you can make the experience of reading the book participatory, interactive, and dynamic.

Reflect questions can also serve as topics of conversation among local groups of teachers or teachers connected electronically in school districts or even between states. Thus, the Reflect items can extend the possibilities for using the books as tools for formal or informal experiences for in-service and preservice teachers, individually or in groups, in or beyond college or university classes.

A new perspective

The Essential Understanding Series thus is intended to support you in gaining a deep and broad understanding of mathematics that can benefit your students in many ways. Considering connections between the mathematics under discussion and other mathematics that students encounter earlier and later in the curriculum gives the books unusual depth as well as insight into vertical articulation in school mathematics.

The series appears against the backdrop of *Principles and Standards for School Mathematics* (NCTM 2000), *Curriculum Focal Points for Prekindergarten through Grade 8 Mathematics: A Quest for Coherence* (NCTM 2006), *Focus in High School Mathematics: Reasoning and Sense Making* (NCTM 2009), and the Navigations Series (NCTM 2001–2009). The new books play an important role, supporting the work of these publications by offering content-based professional development.

The other publications, in turn, can flesh out and enrich the new books. After reading this book, for example, you might select hands-on, Standards-based activities from the Navigations books for your students to use to gain insights into the topics that the Essential Understanding books discuss. If you are teaching students in prekindergarten through grade 8, you might apply your deeper understanding as you present material related to the three focal points that *Curriculum Focal Points* identifies for instruction at your students' level. Or if you are teaching students in grades 9–12, you might use your understanding to enrich the ways in which you can engage students in mathematical reasoning and sense making as presented in *Focus in High School Mathematics: Reasoning and Sense Making.*

An enriched understanding can give you a fresh perspective and infuse new energy into your teaching. We hope that the understanding that you acquire from reading the book will support your efforts as you help your students grasp the ideas that will ensure their mathematical success.

The authors would like to acknowledge the contributions of Hyman Bass, Guershon Harel, Patricio Herbst, and Gabriel Stylianides in providing feedback on the big ideas and essential understandings for this book, as well as the thoughtful reactions to an earlier draft from Shiv Karunakaran, Matt Miller, Meredith Progar, and Michael D. Steele.

Introduction

This book focuses on ideas about proof and proving. These are ideas that you need to understand thoroughly and be able to use flexibly to be highly effective in your teaching of mathematics in grades 9–12. The book discusses many mathematical ideas that are common in high school curricula, and it assumes that you have had a variety of mathematics experiences that have motivated you to delve into—and move beyond—the mathematics that you expect your students to learn.

The book is designed to engage you with these ideas, helping you to develop an understanding that will guide you in planning and implementing lessons and assessing your students' learning in ways that reflect the full complexity of proof and proving. A deep, rich understanding of ideas about these aspects of mathematics will enable you to communicate their importance to your students, showing them how these ideas permeate the mathematics that they have encountered—and will continue to encounter—throughout their school mathematics experiences.

The understanding of proof and proving that you gain from this focused study supports the vision of *Principles and Standards for School Mathematics* (NCTM 2000): "Imagine a classroom, a school, or a school district where all students have access to high-quality, engaging mathematics instruction" (p. 3). This vision depends on classroom teachers such as you, who "are continually growing as professionals" (p. 3) and routinely engage their students in meaningful experiences that help them learn mathematics with understanding.

Why Proof and Proving?

Like the topics of all the volumes in NCTM's Essential Understanding Series, proof and proving are major aspects of school mathematics that are crucial for students to learn but challenging for teachers to teach. Students in grades 9–12 need to engage in proving activities if they are to succeed in these grades and in their subsequent mathematics experiences. Learners often struggle with proving. For example, how do students determine whether a mathematical statement is true or false? Many students rely on a teacher, a textbook, or testing various examples to make this determination. Other students might base their arguments on authority, perception, or popular consensus. To know how statements can be justified (or refuted), it is essential for teachers of grades 9–12 to understand the role of proof in mathematics themselves.

Your work as a teacher of mathematics in these grades calls for a solid understanding of proof and the proving practices that you—and your school, your district, and your state curriculum—expect your students to learn. Your work also requires you to know how this mathematics relates to other mathematical ideas that your students will encounter in the lesson at hand, the current school year, and beyond. Rich mathematical understanding guides teachers' decisions in much of their work, such as choosing tasks for a lesson, posing questions, selecting materials, ordering topics and ideas over time, assessing the quality of students' work, and devising ways to challenge and support their thinking.

Understanding Proof and Proving

Teachers teach mathematics because they want others to understand it in ways that will contribute to success and satisfaction in school, work, and life. In working on any mathematical topic, students need to engage in activities that are part of proving—such as developing conjectures, considering the general case, exploring with examples, looking for structural similarities across cases, and searching for counterexamples. Helping your students to develop their capacity to engage in such activities requires that you understand mathematical reasoning deeply. But what does this mean?

It is easy to think that an understanding of proof and facility in proving as a mathematical process mean knowing why certain things are mathematically appropriate and being able to justify particular theorems. For example, you might be expected to prove particular theorems, understand why a single example does not always prove that a statement is true, or refute claims with a counterexample. You are likely to have encountered tasks that require you to write two-column proofs, paragraph proofs, or proofs by contradiction. You are expected to be skillful in determining whether mathematical statements about the content that you teach are true and whether relevant mathematical terms are used appropriately.

Obviously, facts, vocabulary, and proof techniques are not all that you are expected to know. For example, in your ongoing work with students, you have undoubtedly discovered that not only do you need to know why particular theorems are true, but you are also expected to be able to follow your students' reasoning and justify or refute their claims when appropriate.

It is also easy to focus on a very long list of mathematical ideas that all teachers of mathematics in grades 9–12 are expected to know and teach about proof and proving. Curriculum developers often devise and publish such lists. However important the individual items might be, these lists cannot capture the essence of a rich understanding of the topic. Understanding proof and proving deeply requires you not only to know important mathematical ideas but also to recognize how these ideas relate to one another. Your understanding continues to grow with experience and as a result of opportunities to embrace new ideas and find new connections among familiar ones.

Furthermore, your understanding of proof and proving should transcend the content intended for your students. Some of the differences between what you need to know and what you expect them to learn are easy to point out. For instance, your understanding of the topic should include a grasp of how proof in mathematics differs across algebra, geometry, statistics, and so on, and how proof in mathematics differs from proof in science and in other disciplines.

Other differences between the understanding that you need to have and the understanding that you expect your students to acquire are less obvious, but your experiences in the classroom have undoubtedly made you aware of them at some level. For example, how many times have you been grateful to have an understanding of mathematics that enables you to recognize the merit in a student's unanticipated mathematical question or claim? How many other times have you wondered whether you missed an opportunity to help students refine their arguments because of a gap in your knowledge?

As you have almost certainly discovered, knowing and being able to do familiar mathematics are not enough when you're in the classroom. You also need to be able to identify and justify or refute novel claims. These claims and justifications might draw on ideas or techniques that are beyond the mathematical experiences of your students and current curricular expectations for them, but you might be able to draw on your own knowledge to help students see the merit or flaw in a particular claim.

Big Ideas and Essential Understandings

Thinking about the many particular ideas that are part of a rich understanding of proof and proving can be an overwhelming task. Articulating all of those mathematical ideas and their connections would require many books. To choose which ideas to include in this book, the authors considered a critical question: What is *essential* for teachers of mathematics in grades 9–12 to know about proof and proving to be effective in the classroom? To answer this question, the authors drew on a variety of resources, including personal experiences, the expertise of colleagues in mathematics and mathematics education, and the reactions of reviewers and professional development providers, as well as ideas from curricular materials and research on mathematics learning and teaching.

As a result, the mathematical content of this book focuses on essential ideas for teachers about proof and proving. In particular, chapter 1 is organized around five big ideas related to this important area of mathematics. The big ideas are supported by smaller, more specific mathematical ideas, which the book calls *essential understandings.*

Benefits for Teaching, Learning, and Assessing

Understanding mathematical reasoning can help you implement the Teaching Principle enunciated in *Principles and Standards for School Mathematics*. This Principle sets a high standard for instruction: "Effective mathematics teaching requires understanding what students know and need to learn and then challenging and supporting them to learn it well" (NCTM 2000, p. 16). As in teaching about other critical topics in mathematics, teaching about proof and proving requires knowledge that goes "beyond what most teachers experience in standard preservice mathematics courses" (p. 17).

Chapter 1 comes into play at this point, offering an overview of proof and proving that is intended to be more focused and comprehensive than many discussions of the topic that you are likely to have encountered. This chapter enumerates, expands on, and gives examples of the big ideas and essential understandings related to reasoning, with the goal of supplementing or reinforcing your understanding. Thus, chapter 1 aims to prepare you to implement the Teaching Principle fully as you support and challenge your students in developing more robust proving practices.

Consolidating your understanding in this way also prepares you to implement the Learning Principle outlined in *Principles and Standards*: "Students must learn mathematics with understanding, actively building new knowledge from experience and prior knowledge" (NCTM 2000, p. 20). To support your efforts to help your students learn about proof and proving in this way, chapter 2 builds on the understanding of reasoning that chapter 1 communicates by pointing out specific ways in which the big ideas and essential understandings connect with mathematics that students typically encounter earlier or later in school. This chapter supports the Learning Principle by emphasizing longitudinal connections in students' learning about proof and proving. For example, as their mathematical experiences expand, students understand that there is no mathematical content strand in which proving is not an appropriate activity. The subjects of their proofs and the types of proofs that they produce become more sophisticated as they move through the grades.

The understanding that chapters 1 and 2 convey can strengthen another critical area of teaching. Chapter 3 addresses this area, building on the first two chapters to show how an understanding of proof and proving can help you select and develop appropriate tasks, techniques, and tools for assessing your students' reasoning, facility in conjecturing, and skill in constructing arguments. An ownership of the big ideas and essential understandings related to proof and proving, reinforced by an understanding of students' past and future experiences with mathematical reasoning, can help you ensure that assessment in your classroom supports the development of understanding of proof and skill in proving.

Such assessment satisfies the first requirement of the Assessment Principle set out in *Principles and Standards*: "Assessment should support the learning of important mathematics and furnish useful information to both teachers and students" (NCTM 2000, p. 22). An understanding of proof and proving can also help you satisfy the second requirement of the Assessment Principle, by enabling you to develop assessment tasks that give you specific information about how your students are reasoning and what they understand. For example, a proof task might ask students to evaluate two arguments. One argument might be an algebraic proof, and the other argument might be based on examples, with the prompt worded in such a way to leave open the possibility that both arguments were valid. Students could discuss not only whether the given arguments were valid proofs but also provide reasons why or why not. They could be asked to write a paragraph discussing whether the arguments were valid proofs, with the possibility that both arguments were valid. This would increase the likelihood that students would not choose an argument just because it had more words or more symbols.

Ready to Begin

This introduction has painted the background, preparing you for the big ideas and associated essential understandings related to proof and proving that you will encounter and explore in chapter 1. Reading the chapters in the order in which they appear can be a very useful way to approach the book. Read chapter 1 in more than one sitting, allowing time for reflection. Absorb the ideas—both big ideas and essential understandings—related to proof and proving. Appreciate the connections among these ideas. Carry your newfound or reinforced understanding to chapter 2, which guides you in seeing how the ideas related to reasoning are connected to the mathematics that your students have encountered earlier or will encounter later in school. Then read about teaching, learning, and assessment issues in chapter 3.

Alternatively, you may want to take a look at chapter 3 before engaging with the mathematical ideas in chapters 1 and 2. Having the challenges of teaching, learning, and assessment issues clearly in mind, along with possible approaches to them, can give you a different perspective on the material in the earlier chapters.

No matter how you read the book, let it serve as a tool to expand your understanding, application, and enjoyment of proof and proving.

Chapter 1

Proof and Proving: The Big Ideas and Essential Understandings

The aim of this book is to build your knowledge of mathematical proof to support you as you develop your students' reasoning and proof practices in your classroom. Proof occurs as an integral part of every strand of 9–12 mathematics and progresses across the high school years. Proof and proving are fundamental parts of reasoning mathematically; any engagement in authentic mathematical reasoning must involve the related activities of developing proofs, making sense of existing proofs, refuting invalid arguments, and engaging in proof and argumentation as routine parts of doing mathematics. As you read through the following chapters, you will learn more about these related activities and how they constitute critical aspects of mathematics.

Proof is central to the practice of mathematicians, and to engage students in genuine mathematical activity, teachers should make it central to 9–12 mathematics. Mathematicians contend that proof is one of the defining characteristics of mathematics and that the very essence of mathematics lies in proofs. Moreover, many have argued that the process of proving is the one aspect of mathematics "that most clearly distinguishes mathematical behavior from scientific behavior in other disciplines" (Dreyfus 1990, p. 126). From a mathematician's perspective, proof cannot be separated from the rest of mathematics. However, it is all too commonly a separate part of the curriculum in 9–12 mathematics. In the most extreme cases, proof may occur only in a high school geometry class, and even then as a separate activity, after students have already learned the necessary theorems and postulates. Even if proof does occur in other mathematics courses, all too often it is relegated to a separate unit or to a series of bonus activities for the more advanced students.

According to mathematics educator Alan Schoenfeld (1994), "proof is not a thing separable from mathematics, as it appears to be in our curricula; it is an essential component of doing, communicating, and recording mathematics. And I believe it can be embedded in our curricula, at all levels" (p. 76). We agree with Schoenfeld's claim and will discuss ways to think about proof as an integral part of every mathematics course. Throughout this book, we focus on the central activities involved in proof and proving, and we show how these activities can be made a key part of mathematical learning and problem solving at any level and in any content area.

Five Big Ideas and Related Essential Understandings

In the remainder of this chapter, we focus on five interrelated big ideas and fourteen associated essential understandings that support the big ideas. The big ideas highlight what it means to prove, what the goals of proof are, what roles proof can play in mathematics learning, and what the central nature of proof is in 9–12 mathematics. The essential understandings further develop each of the big ideas, unpacking the meanings, forms, and purposes of proof that are important for teaching in grades 9–12. These are ideas that teachers need to understand thoroughly and be able to use flexibly to support their students' development of proof specifically and mathematical reasoning more generally.

The big ideas and essential understandings are identified as a group below to give you a quick overview and for your convenience in referring back to them later. Read through them now, but do not think that you must absorb them fully at this point. The chapter will discuss each one in turn in detail.

Big Idea 1. Proof is part and parcel of doing mathematics and should be a regular and ongoing part of the learning of mathematics.

> **Essential Understanding 1a.** The processes of proving include a variety of activities, such as developing conjectures, considering the general case, exploring with examples, looking for structural similarities across cases, and searching for counterexamples.

> **Essential Understanding 1b.** Making sense of others' arguments and determining their validity are proof-related activities.

Big Idea 2.
A proof is a specific type of mathematical argument, which is a connected sequence of deductive, logical statements in support of or against a mathematical claim.

> **Essential Understanding 2a.** A proof uses definitions and statements that are true and available without further justification.

> **Essential Understanding 2b.** Many modes of argumentation are valid for engaging in proving or disproving statements, including deductive processes such as mathematical induction, as well as finding counterexamples.

> **Essential Understanding 2c.** A proof can have many different valid representational forms, including narrative, picture, diagram, two-column presentation, or algebraic form.

Big Idea 3.
A proof demonstrates the truth of a statement beyond any doubt for all possible cases.

> **Essential Understanding 3a.** The truth of a proved statement is dependent on the original definitions, axioms, and theorems on which the proof relies.

> **Essential Understanding 3b.** Once a statement has been proved, finding a counterexample is not possible.

Big Idea 4.
A proof is not an argument based on authority, perception, popular consensus, intuition, probability, or examples.

> **Essential Understanding 4a.** The idea of proof in mathematics is unique and differs in notable ways from the notion of proof in science and other disciplines.

> **Essential Understanding 4b.** Examples can be a critical part of the proving process but do not suffice as a mathematical proof, except in the case of proof by exhaustion or proof by counterexample.

Big Idea 5.
Proof has many different roles in mathematics.

> **Essential Understanding 5a.** One role of proof is to verify the truth or falsehood of a statement.

> **Essential Understanding 5b.** Proof can provide insight into why a statement is true.

> **Essential Understanding 5c.** Proofs can provide an entry point for the development of a new theory or idea.

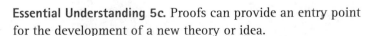

Essential Understanding 5d. Proofs create an appropriate structure for communicating mathematical knowledge.

Essential Understanding 5e. Proofs provide an impetus for the use of precise mathematical language.

Proof Is an Integral Part of Mathematics: Big Idea 1

Big Idea 1. *Proof is part and parcel of doing mathematics and should be a regular and ongoing part of the learning of mathematics.*

When people think of proof in mathematics, they may remember geometry class in high school and two-column proofs. Traditionally, proof was relegated to geometry and not visited again until post-calculus college mathematics. However, this trend began to reverse in 2000 when the National Council of Teachers of Mathematics (NCTM) published *Principles and Standards for School Mathematics*, specifically highlighting the importance of deductive reasoning at all levels of mathematics: "Reasoning and proof should be a consistent part of students' mathematical experience in prekindergarten through grade 12. Reasoning mathematically is a habit of mind, and like all habits, it must be developed through consistent use in many contexts" (2000, p. 56). These recommendations reflect an understanding that proof is a fundamental aspect of what it means to reason mathematically. Regardless of the content area, class, or level in 9–12 mathematics, proof should be a regular part of every student's mathematical experience.

Everyday math activities can be occasions for proving

At first glance, many aspects of mathematics might not seem to involve proof. For instance, consider an algebra activity called "Distance to Horizon" at NCTM's Illuminations website. In this activity, students learn that the distance to the horizon is the distance from their eye to the point of tangency formed by the tangent line from their eye to the surface of the earth. As their height above the earth increases, the horizon appears farther away. Students can explore this idea with an applet that simultaneously measures the height above sea level and the distance to the horizon (see fig. 1.1a). As students use the applet, they can collect data to compare the distances to the horizon for multiple heights. For instance, students might create a table with heights (in feet) and distances (in miles), as shown in figure 1.1b.

The Illuminations lesson "Distance to Horizon" is available at http://illuminations.nctm.org/ActivityDetail.aspx?ID=150.

One of the tasks in the activity asks students, "Can you find a rule that will allow you to predict the distance y to the horizon (in miles), if you know your height x (in feet) above sea level?" Suppose that one group of students decides to plot multiple points to see what a graph of the relationship might look like (see fig. 1.2).

After looking at the graph, several students remark that it looks like a square root function. To test this observation, the students take

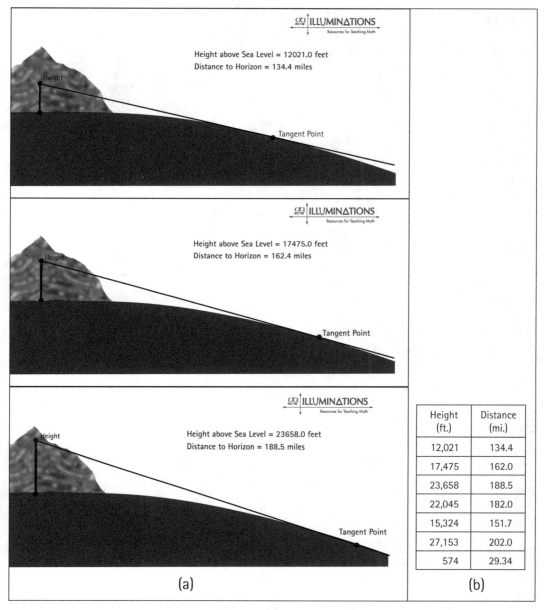

Height above Sea Level = 12021.0 feet
Distance to Horizon = 134.4 miles

Tangent Point

Height above Sea Level = 17475.0 feet
Distance to Horizon = 162.4 miles

Tangent Point

Height above Sea Level = 23658.0 feet
Distance to Horizon = 188.5 miles

Tangent Point

Height (ft.)	Distance (mi.)
12,021	134.4
17,475	162.0
23,658	188.5
22,045	182.0
15,324	151.7
27,153	202.0
574	29.34

(a)   (b)

Fig. 1.1. NCTM Illuminations applet for the activity "Distance to Horizon" and a student-made table

the square of the y-values in their table. For instance, they transform the point (574, 29.34) into (574, 860.8), which they round to (574, 861). Then a student notices, "861 is just 574 times 1.5!" The students then try the same technique with all of the other points, multiplying the x-value by 1.5 and then taking the square root, and they find that each time they get the correct y-value. They are then able to create the equation and graph the function, as shown in figure 1.3. Reflect 1.1 invites you to consider the students' solution.

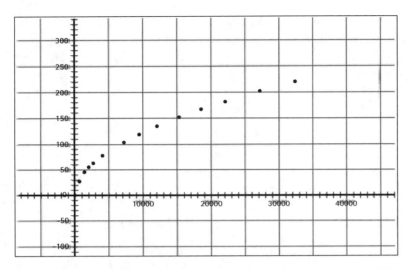

Fig. 1.2. Graph of points representing the relationship between height and distance to horizon

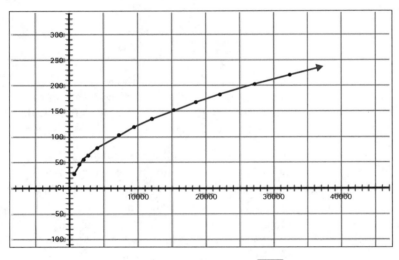

Fig. 1.3. Graph of $y = \sqrt{1.5x}$

Reflect 1.1

Do you think the students' solution was mathematically appropriate? Why would it make sense that the function would be a square root function?

In a typical algebra class, the activity might end here, or it might serve as a launching point for investigating features of square root functions. But this activity also presents a proof opportunity. In particular, why can the distance to the horizon be represented by $y = \sqrt{1.5x}$ for a height of x feet? Why should there be a square root in the equation for y?

One way to think about the applet's diagram is in terms of the earth's circumference as modeled by a circle. A teacher could introduce an alternate diagram, such as the one in figure 1.4, and ask students to use it to justify their method for determining y in their table of values. In the figure below, y is the distance to horizon, x is the height, and R is the radius of the earth.

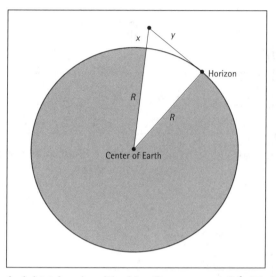

Fig. 1.4. A right triangle with sides $R + x$, y, and R (with R as the earth's radius, x as the height above the earth's surface, and y as the distance to the horizon)

Because the triangle is a right triangle, it is possible to use the Pythagorean theorem to calculate the value of y. Students can use the Pythagorean theorem to write $R^2 + y^2 = (R + x)^2$, which they can transform to $y = \sqrt{x(2Rx + x)}$. For heights that are close to the surface of the earth (such as views from a mountain, building, or hot air balloon), the value of x is negligible compared with the value of R (that is, the ratio x to R is very close to zero). Therefore, one can disregard the x in the sum $2R + x$. Students can then engage in appropriate conversions between feet and miles to find that $y = \sqrt{2Rx}$ is approximately equal to $y = \sqrt{1.5x}$.

To engage students in authentic mathematical activity, teachers should make proof a part of mathematical investigation and problem solving. Understanding why $y = \sqrt{1.5x}$ is a valid way to calculate the distance to the horizon can help students make connections between algebra and geometry, engage in multiple approaches to developing the square root function, and make meaningful shifts across representational forms. Engaging in the act of proof, therefore, can help students gain a better understanding of the mathematical content and make new connections. Proof is a critical tool for making sense of the mathematics that we learn; thus, it should be a fundamental part of every math class, not just geometry.

For additional discussion of transforming equations in meaningful ways, see *Developing Essential Understanding of Expressions, Equations, and Functions for Teaching Mathematics in Grades 6–8* (Lloyd, Herbel-Eisenmann, and Star 2011).

Some people might think of proof as a sophisticated form of reasoning that only advanced students in the upper grades can handle. However, all students can and should engage in proving; it is not something to reserve for the best students in the class. Throughout this book, we will provide examples of many different types of proofs that are produced by students at different grade levels and in different classes and that represent different degrees of correctness and sophistication. Although a beginning algebra student may not necessarily produce the most polished or elegant proof, this does not mean that proving is an activity that is too sophisticated for less advanced students. Students at all levels can engage in deductive reasoning, and this is a type of reasoning that will become more natural to students the more they do it.

Proof can involve many activities

Essential Understanding 1a. *The processes of proving include a variety of activities, such as developing conjectures, considering the general case, exploring with examples, looking for structural similarities across cases, and searching for counterexamples.*

Proving as a process involves a kind of higher-order thinking that is not that different from that required for problem solving. When mathematicians learn about new theorems, read new proofs, or engage in mathematical investigations, they naturally develop conjectures as a result of their explorations. However, how often are students in grades 9–12 given those types of opportunities to play with mathematical ideas? Not often, for the most part; instead, students are usually presented with existing statements that they have to prove. This means that students are expected to jump right into the proof process without having any opportunities to explore a conjecture, examine different possibilities, try different examples, think about a conjecture's limitations, or otherwise gain a solid understanding of the idea that they are supposed to prove.

The process of proving does not have to start with a given statement and an attempt at a formal proof right off the bat. Instead, the process of proving can be much more open, creative, and messy. It can include developing conjectures, exploring many different examples, thinking about potential counterexamples, trying to find patterns and understand why they exist, and engaging in other open-ended explorations. Engaging students in mathematical proof should therefore be aimed not only at developing their capacities to generate a proof as an end in itself, but also at providing students with opportunities to develop a host of skills that they can use in a variety of non-proof-related tasks. For instance, consider the Finding Slopes problem:

Finding Slopes

The *slope* of a linear function is the rate of change in the independent variable for a unit change in the dependent variable. There are several ways to describe how to find slope:

- "Rise over run"

- "Change in *y* over change in *x*"

- $\dfrac{y_2 - y_1}{x_2 - x_1}$

Describe *why* each of these methods can be used to find slope. Discuss similarities and differences among the methods, including situations where one method would be preferred over another method.

Reflect 1.2 extends these ideas about slope to other families of functions.

Reflect 1.2

The term *slope* is used to describe the constant rate of change in the *y*-variable for each unit of change in the *x*-variable for the linear functions. The greater the absolute value of the slope, the more "steep" a line will appear to be.

What about *nonlinear* functions? Do aspects of quadratic, cubic, or even quartic functions have "slope-like" properties? How do these properties of nonlinear functions differ from the concept of *slope*?

See *Developing Essential Understanding of Functions for Teaching Mathematics in Grades 9–12* (Cooney, Beckmann, and Lloyd 2010) for further discussion of slope and other families of functions.

Ideas about slope are standard introductory algebra content. The Finding Slopes problem offers a richer exploration of slope by pressing students not only to argue why each method yields a rate that is equivalent to the slope of a line, but also to consider similarities and differences in the methods and whether there are situations in which one method might be preferred over another. When students are engaged in these tasks, they discover that doing mathematics is more than just learning a procedure and applying it. Mathematical thinking involves recognizing similarities and differences in general features of procedures and processes. Developing the habit of recognizing such similarities and differences, even when learning about new procedures, supports students in generating mathematical conjectures.

For example, to argue why finding the "rise over run" of a line will yield the slope of the linear equation, a student first needs to articulate what is meant by "rise" and "run." This work leads to the discovery of connections with the other methods, as well as a key difference, when considering linear equations with negative slope. Investigating similarities (and differences) among cases is a valuable step in generating mathematical conjectures. In the process of understanding the mathematical features that apply to a general case, similarities between cases become more salient than differences.

One similarity among all methods for finding slope involves relating the change in y-values to the change in x-values, also described as finding a ratio of change in y to the change in x. The methods given in the Finding Slopes problem differ in how this ratio is described; the phrase "rise over run" describes a method of finding slope that is related specifically to the graphical representation of a line, whereas the method of finding slope as $\frac{y_2 - y_1}{x_2 - x_1}$ can be used in situations where only two points of the line are known.

It is important to design activities in which students compare and contrast mathematical ideas such as computational procedures and generate conjectures as to why procedures are valid. Exploring how those conjectures work with examples deepens students' understanding of situations in which procedures can be used and how they work mathematically. More important, designing activities that engage students in a variety of proof-related activities builds habits of mind that cannot develop if students encounter proof-related tasks only when they must prove a given conjecture. The processes involved in generating and proving conjectures call on students to use valuable problem-solving skills, such as generating representations of complex ideas, which apply to a variety of mathematical tasks beyond generating proof (Weber 2005).

Evaluating others' arguments is an important proof-related activity

Essential Understanding 1b. *Making sense of others' arguments and determining their validity are proof-related activities.*

As we discussed in relation to Essential Understanding 1*a*, proving is not limited to the creation of a formal written proof; many of the activities leading up to writing a proof are part of the proving process. Another aspect of proof involves making sense of existing proofs and determining whether another person's argument is valid or invalid. An important part of mathematical proficiency is the ability to distinguish correct reasoning from flawed reasoning. We can foster these skills by challenging students to judge the appropriateness of arguments. For instance, consider the following reasoning from students in response to a problem about exponential growth:

Essential Understanding 1a
The processes of proving include a variety of activities, such as developing conjectures, considering the general case, exploring with examples, looking for structural similarities across cases, and searching for counterexamples.

Jactus Growth

If the height of a Jactus plant doubles every day, how much does it grow every week? Make a table to show the Jactus plant's growth.

Two students, Uditi and Jill, decide to create different tables to use in exploring the problem. Because the problem does not specify how tall the Jactus plant is at the outset, Uditi decides to create a table for a plant that is initially 1 inch tall, and Jill makes a table for a plant that is initially 2 inches tall. The students are curious about whether the plant will grow the same amount in one week, regardless of its initial height. Uditi's work is shown in figure 1.5.

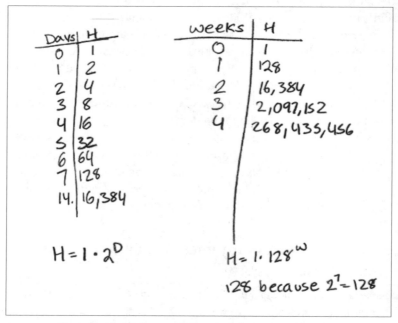

Fig. 1.5. Uditi's work on the Jactus Growth problem

Uditi decides that the plant will grow 128 times as tall as its initial height in 1 week. She creates a table for the plant's height each day, and then another table for the plant's height each week, and explains that 2 to the seventh power is 128: "There are, like, 7 days in a week, and I do times 2, then times 2, times 2 ... to get the next number, so it's 2 times 2 times 2, so it goes on for 7 for 1 week." Jill then realizes that she has the same result, even though she started her table with an initial height of 2 inches. At day 7, her Jactus plant is 256 inches tall, which is 128 times the initial height of the plant.

This realization could lead to a conjecture: "If a plant doubles in height every day, then it will always grow to be 128 times as tall in 1 week, regardless of its initial height." One could create several different arguments to support such a conjecture. As suggested in

Reflect 1.3, think about the types of arguments that you would want your students to make.

Reflect 1.3

What types of arguments would you like to see from your students to justify the conjecture that doubling every day will lead to growing 128 times as tall in 1 week? Think about the different ways in which one could justify this statement.

Consider the following three arguments about the Jactus plant's growth. Do Amala, Mila, and Caleb make the types of arguments that you would like (or expect) your students to make?

Argument 1: Amala decides to test multiple cases. She creates tables in which the initial height of the plant is 1 inch, 2 inches, 5 inches, and ½ inch. Using a table in which the initial height is 5 inches (see fig. 1.6), she argues for the growth always being 128 times the initial height: "I did the same thing with every table, so I will just use this one as an example. The plant starts at 5 inches tall. After 7 days, it is 640 inches tall, which is 128 times 5. Then I kept going. After another week, on day 14, it was 81,920 inches tall, and if you divide that by 640 you get 128 again. You can just keep going, and the pattern will continue. It always gets 128 times bigger every 7 days, and it doesn't really matter what the starting height is because you can just compensate by dividing by the starting height value. So for the table where the starting height is 2 inches, after 7 days it's 256 inches, but if you divide that by 2, it's 128. So here the equation is $y = 5 \cdot 2^x$, and x is for days. The only thing that will change in your equation is that starting height."

Argument 2: Mila decides to reason about the algebraic expressions in the problem: "If the height doubles every day, you can just write that as $y = 2^x$, and x stands for days. So if you want to convert it to weeks, there are 7 days in a week, so you could write it as $y = 2^{7x}$. But 2^7 is just 128, so that's why it gets 128 times as big each week. It doesn't matter what the starting height is because that doesn't change the expression $y = 2^{7x}$."

Argument 3: Caleb argues that you can think about a general plant of height H: "Let's just imagine that the plant is H inches tall when it starts growing. It really doesn't matter what H is. Then, after 1 day, the plant doubles.

So it's 2*H*. Then after 2 days, the plant doubles again, so it's 4*H*. Then it doubles to 8*H*, then 16*H*, then 32*H*, then 64*H*, then 128*H* after 7 days. So after 1 week it will have grown to 128*H*, and if you divide that by *H*, you get 128. So it doesn't matter what *H* is."

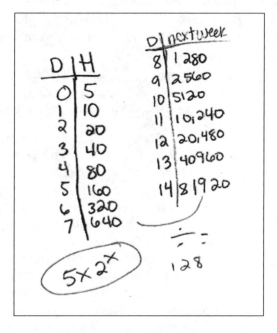

Fig. 1.6. Amala's table of growth for a Jactus plant with an initial height of 5 inches

Take some time to evaluate the three arguments. The questions in Reflect 1.4 might guide your critique.

Reflect 1.4

Do you think any of the three arguments is valid? What are the arguments' limitations?

What aspects of the arguments represent appropriate mathematical reasoning? How could you use the ideas expressed in the arguments to generate new conjectures?

Students should be able to make sense of one another's arguments, regardless of the arguments' correctness, as well as of more standard proofs that they encounter in their textbooks or receive from their teachers. In this case, examining the validity of each of the three arguments could open up a number of important areas for discussion and understanding. For instance, analysis might prompt a question about the role of a generic example (Balacheff 1987) in the argument and whether the "starting at 5 inches" table fills that role appropriately. Why is it valid to argue that $y = 2^{7x}$ is equivalent to $y = 128^x$, and how can this be justified with the laws of exponents? Do any elements of these arguments suggest a more general phenomenon about exponential growth?

Making sense of others' arguments and determining their validity can help students develop new ideas about the mathematical content at hand and can also support their generation of new conjectures, discovery of new relationships, and development of new ideas. Distinct skills come into play in generating, as opposed to understanding, proofs, and the ability to make sense of proofs and arguments is no less important than the ability to write a proof. Providing students with opportunities to evaluate existing arguments can be an important way to support the development of their abilities to create proofs (Ellis 2011; Knuth, Choppin, and Bieda 2009).

Proof as Mathematical Argument: Big Idea 2

Big Idea 2. *A proof is a specific type of mathematical argument, which is a connected sequence of deductive, logical statements in support of or against a mathematical claim.*

In school mathematics, where students learn to use mathematics in academic as well as applied settings, what do we actually mean by *proof*? A number of definitions have been used in developing mathematics education policy, in doing research on the teaching and learning of mathematical proof, and in writing school mathematics textbooks. A sample of the definitions of *proof* that have been used for these purposes appears below:

- Proofs are "arguments consisting of logically rigorous deductions of conclusions from hypotheses" (NCTM 2000, p. 55).

- *Proof* is a *mathematical argument*, a connected sequence of assertions for or against a mathematical claim, with the following characteristics:

  1. It uses statements accepted by the classroom community (*set of accepted statements*) that are true and available without further justification;

  2. It employs forms of reasoning (*modes of argumentation*) that are known to, or within the conceptual reach of, the classroom community; and

  3. It is communicated with forms of expression (*modes of argument representation*) that are appropriate and known to, or within the conceptual reach of, the classroom community. (Stylianides 2007, p. 291; italics in original)

- A proof is a finite sequence of formulae of some given system, and each formula of the sequence is either an axiom of the system or a formula derived by a rule of the system from some of the preceding formulae. (Lakatos 1998, p. 155)

Reflect 1.5 provides an opportunity to compare these definitions of *proof*.

Reflect 1.5

What features do the definitions of *proof* given by NCTM, Stylianides, and Lakatos have in common? Do you know other definitions of *mathematical proof*? How do those definitions compare with the ones given above? Which definition most closely describes proof as it occurs in your classroom?

Although these definitions of *proof* emphasize different aspects of the proving process, such as the use of axioms and rules or the involvement of the classroom community, common elements appear in all three definitions. First, each definition describes proof as an argument, or consisting of mathematical arguments. A proof goes beyond making a claim. A proof consists of a mathematical argument or arguments to support or refute a claim. Second, each definition indicates that proofs are constructed from given statements, conclusions, axioms, or facts that act as building blocks in generating a mathematical argument. If students do not know or understand these building blocks, they will not be able to construct a proof.

Consider the following proof of the claim that the sum of the angle measures of any quadrilateral in planar geometry is 360 degrees (see fig. 1.7a):

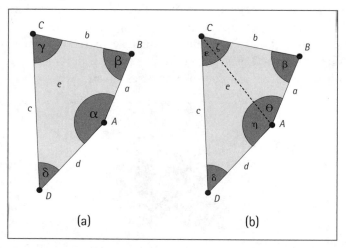

(a)   (b)

Fig. 1.7. (a) A general quadrilateral and (b) the same quadrilateral with segment *AC*

Given: Figure *CDAB* is a quadrilateral.

Prove: Construct a segment between points *C* and *A* (see fig. 1.7b). Then $\gamma = \varepsilon + \xi$ and $\alpha = \eta + \theta$.

By the triangle sum theorem (all angles of a triangle sum to 180 degrees), $\delta + \eta + \varepsilon = 180°$ and $\theta + \xi + \beta = 180°$. Therefore, $\theta + \xi + \beta + \delta + \eta + \varepsilon = 360°$. So, the sum of the angle measures of a quadrilateral is 360 degrees.

The basic elements of mathematical proof are at play in the proof of the quadrilateral sum theorem. First, the proof is making a mathematical argument to support a claim that the sum of the angle measures of any quadrilateral in planar geometry is 360 degrees.

Second, the proof is constructed from axioms, accepted statements, and theorems—in particular, the first axiom of Euclid's *Elements* ("For any two distinct points P and Q, there is a unique line containing them"), which allowed for the construction of a line segment between points A and C; the triangle sum theorem; and the additive property of equality (since $\delta + \eta + \varepsilon = 180°$ and $\theta + \xi + \beta = 180°$, then $\theta + \xi + \beta + \delta + \eta + \varepsilon = 180° + 180°$).

Proof is more than just mathematical reasoning. Students can explain their mathematical thinking without engaging in proof, as well as produce less polished proofs that serve as justifications for mathematical claims but fall short of functioning as proofs. For example, a student may reason that the sum of the measures of the angles of a quadrilateral is 360 degrees by constructing several quadrilaterals on paper, cutting or tearing the sheets of paper so that each quadrilateral separates into four pieces, and then placing the angles in a circular pattern to illustrate that the angles can be configured to make 360 degrees, as in figure 1.8. This activity shows physically that for the quadrilaterals constructed, the angle measures sum to 360 degrees, but it falls short of proving the statement because it relies on the specific cases constructed.

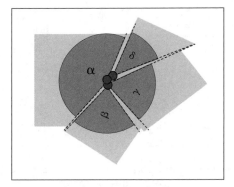

Fig. 1.8. Illustrating the sum of the interior angles of a quadrilateral

Although activities such as explaining, justifying, and informally proving can build a foundational understanding that supports students in engaging in proving, proof is a specific kind of mathematical activity that establishes truth (or refutes claims) in the discipline of mathematics. The essential understandings associated with Big Idea 2 address the specific activity of proof as distinct from other kinds of activity related to mathematical reasoning.

Proof relies on true statements and assumptions

Essential Understanding 2a. A proof uses definitions and statements that are true and available without further justification.

Proofs rely on the use of available definitions, axioms, and already-proved theorems. Creating and understanding definitions are essential aspects of the capacity to prove, as is understanding the role that axioms play as the building blocks of proof. A proof's validity relies on the definitions and axioms on which it is built.

The role of definitions

Definitions play an important role in proving because they set the boundaries for what theorems apply to the mathematical objects involved in a given conjecture. Defining is a significant mathematical activity: students' recognition of the importance of understanding and applying definitions is a key conceptual pivot point in the development of their capacities to prove. However, according to Herbst, Gonzalez, and Macke (2005), students initially have difficulties in reconciling mathematical definitions with definitions of words. Whereas words are taught by providing definitions elaborated with connections to synonyms and antonyms as well as examples of the words used in context, a mathematical definition is "the statement of the necessary and sufficient conditions that an object must meet to be labeled by a certain word or expression" (p. 17).

Herbst, Gonzalez, and Macke (2005) emphasize the following aspects of creating and using definitions in mathematics: (1) definitions are characterized by succinctness; (2) alternative definitions can highlight different properties of the same mathematical object; and (3) choosing a definition determines what theorems can be used to prove, as well as how they can be used in a proof. A proof depends on the provers' understanding and use of definitions to support their work in developing a proof, so a part of learning to prove involves learning to construct and interpret mathematically useful definitions. Reflect 1.6 illustrates the importance of attending to the meaning and precision of definitions when proving.

See *Developing Essential Understanding of Geometry for Teaching Mathematics in Grades 9–12* (Sinclair, Pimm, and Skelin 2012) for an extensive discussion of the centrality of definitions in geometry.

Reflect 1.6

One definition that has historically been debated in mathematics is the definition of a trapezoid. Consider the following two definitions of *trapezoid*: (1) a quadrilateral having two, and only two, sides parallel, and (2) a quadrilateral having at least two sides parallel.

Given the statement, "A parallelogram is a trapezoid," which definition could you use to prove (or disprove) the statement?

The role of axioms and assumptions

Understanding proof involves recognizing that axioms cannot be proven within the given system. The notion that there exists a whole number 0 is an axiom, and Euclidean geometry was built on five postulates (axioms), such as the notion that a unique straight line exists between two points. Axioms are essential building blocks of mathematical systems, such as Euclidean geometry and real numbers.

Bell (1976) emphasizes the role of proof in systematizing mathematical knowledge into a "deductive system of axioms, major concepts and theorems, and minor results derived from these" (p. 24). In the case of pre-K–12 mathematics, this would involve both identifying assumptions and understanding that, in the given context, each assumption is either an accepted basic principle (axiom) or can itself be proven on the basis of other, more basic, assumptions. Attending to, making explicit, and discussing what is taken as axiomatic is an overlooked part of learning to prove. Consider the following proof that $\dfrac{x^2-1}{x-1} = x + 1$:

Proof. Because $x^2 - 1 = (x-1)(x+1)$, then $\dfrac{x^2-1}{x-1} = \dfrac{(x-1)(x+1)}{x-1}$,

which can be rewritten as $\dfrac{(x-1)}{(x-1)} \cdot \dfrac{(x+1)}{1}$. Because any number

divided by itself is 1, then $\dfrac{(x-1)(x+1)}{x-1} = \dfrac{(x+1)}{1}$.

A number of assumptions, some true and some false, are at play in this erroneous proof. When $x = 1$ or $x = -1$, $x^2 - 1 = 0$, so the step of factoring the numerator can be completed, by the factor theorem. However, because x is a variable that could be 1, and so possibly $x - 1$ could be 0, the axiom that for any nonzero number n, $\dfrac{n}{n} = 1$, could not be applied in the third step of the proof, since division of nonzero numbers by 0 is undefined. A proof is valid only if the assumptions on which it relies are true. Developing the capacity to rigorously question all assumptions when developing mathematical justifications is a key mathematical habit of mind.

Proofs can rely on a variety of modes of argumentation

Essential Understanding 2b. *Many modes of argumentation are valid for engaging in proving and disproving statements, including deductive processes such as mathematical induction, as well as finding counterexamples.*

Proof relies on no one standard way of constructing an argument. Often, it is easier to use a particular mode of argumentation, depending on the nature of the claim, but other modes of argumentation may be used to construct a proof. Take the statement that the sum of n natural numbers $(1 + 2 + 3 + ... n)$ equals $\dfrac{n(n+1)}{2}$. A common belief is that when the famous mathematician Carl Friedrich Gauss (1777–1855) was a schoolchild, he found the sum of the first 100 numbers in a matter of minutes by generating the following sequence of sums:

$$100 + 1$$
$$99 + 2$$
$$98 + 3$$
$$\vdots$$
$$52 + 49$$
$$51 + 50$$

Gauss supposedly realized that there were 50 such pairs, so the sum would be $\dfrac{100(101)}{2}$. He had deduced the formula for the sum of n natural numbers, $S = \dfrac{n(n+1)}{2}$, and his method could be represented as a general, deductive symbolic proof:

Let $S = 1 + 2 + 3 + ... + (n - 1) + n$.
Then, $2S = 1 + 2 + 3 + ... + (n - 1) + n + n + (n - 1) + ... + 3 + 2 + 1$.
Pairing terms, $2S = (1 + n) + (2 + n - 1) + (3 + n - 2) + ... + (n - 2 + 3) + (n - 1 + 2) + (n + 1)$
$$= (1 + n) + (1 + n) + (1 + n) + ... + (n + 1) + (n + 1) + (n + 1)$$
$$= n(n + 1).$$
Therefore, $S = \dfrac{n(n+1)}{2}$.

A visual proof can also be constructed to show the sum of n natural numbers. In figure 1.9, the white squares represent the sum $1 + 2 + 3 + 4 + 5 + 6 + 7 + 8 + 9 + 10$. The area of the whole rectangle is $10 \cdot 11$, or 110, square units. To get the area, or the sum, of just the white squares or the olive squares, we would compute $\dfrac{10 \cdot 11}{2} = 55$ units. By adding or deleting rows of unit squares, thus increasing or decreasing the vertical or horizontal dimension of the rectangle, we could construct such a picture for the sum of any *n* natural numbers.

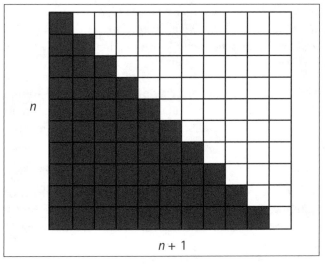

Fig. 1.9. An *n* by (*n* + 1) rectangle for a pictorial proof

In some instances, statements cannot be proven by all modes of argumentation but may be limited to a few or even one specific mode. For example, consider the following claim: "There are 20 ways to create a flag with 2 colors out of a total of 5 color choices (order matters)." We have only a finite number of cases to consider, since there are only 5 possible color choices, and the flag contains only two colors. A proof by exhaustion is appropriate because we need only to show systematically that there are just 20 possibilities by listing all possible color combinations. However, for some conjectures, producing such a list would take a mathematician—or even a team of mathematicians—longer than a lifetime to produce. The famous four-color theorem is one such statement, and after more than a hundred years of unsuccessful attempts to prove the claim by using different methods of proof, mathematicians finally proved it by using supercomputers to list all possible color combinations.

In contrast, it would be impossible to test all cases to prove the statement, "The sum of two consecutive odd numbers is divisible by 4," because the domain to which the statement applies is the infinite set of all real numbers. A proof by counterexample would also be inappropriate, because the statement happens to be true! Some possible approaches would be a proof by deduction, proof by induction, or proof by contradiction. However, in attempting a proof, some approaches may be easier to use than others. Mathematicians will revisit the proof of a theorem if they believe that a different mode of argumentation will lead to a simpler or more elegant proof.

Some claims lend themselves to particular modes of argumentation, whereas other claims consume a mathematician's career to

The four-color theorem states that no more than four colors are needed to color the regions of any map with no two adjacent regions having the same color.

find an acceptable proof. Fermat's famous last theorem—that no three positive integers a, b, and c can satisfy the equation $a^n + b^n = c^n$ for any integer value of n greater than 2—occupied mathematicians for centuries until the advent of mathematical discoveries that could be used to prove it. The next essential understanding underscores the fact that in the same way that many modes of argumentation can be used when proving, many representational forms can be used to generate a valid mathematical proof.

Proofs can take many representational forms

Essential Understanding 2c. *A proof can have many different valid representational forms, including narrative, picture, diagram, two-column, or algebraic form.*

Typically, the phrase "mathematical proof" conjures images of the two-column proof form common in a traditional high school geometry curriculum. In the two-column form, the statements composing the proof are written in the left column, and the justifications, or reasons for using the statements, are provided in the right column. One advantage of such a representation is that it makes explicit the axioms and theorems that the prover is assuming to be true to carry out the proof. A proof of $(x + y)^2 = x^2 + 2xy + y^2$ can take a written form similar to a two-column proof by listing reasons, such as applying the definition of *exponent* and the distributive property, after each step in manipulating variables on the left-hand side of the equation. However, consider the picture in figure 1.10 as a pictorial proof.

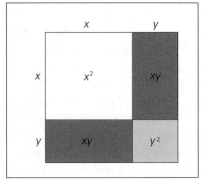

Fig. 1.10. A pictorial proof of the product of a binomial squared

Does the picture prove that $(x + y)^2 = x^2 + 2xy + y^2$? It is clearly a shape with dimensions that are limited to the physical space afforded by the medium in which we are representing the shape. But are the dimensions of x and y sufficiently arbitrary for the picture to count as a proof? Even mathematicians have generated pictures for some well-known theorems; the twelfth-century

Hindu mathematician Bhaskara produced a visual proof of the Pythagorean theorem, as shown in figure 1.11.

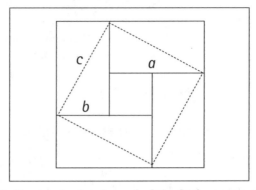

Fig. 1.11. Bhaskara's visual proof of the Pythagorean theorem. (Retrieved from http://www.cut-the-knot.org/pythagoras/index.shtml.)

In Bhaskara's picture, a tilted square has been formed by using four congruent right triangles, with the length of the hypotenuse as c, the length of the longer leg as a, and the length of the shorter leg as b. A smaller square, in the center of the picture, has side length $a - b$. The tilted square has area c^2, and each of the triangles has area $\frac{1}{2}ab$. The area of the small square is $(a - b)^2$. So,

$$(a - b)^2 = c^2 - 4 \cdot \left(\frac{1}{2}ab\right)$$
$$(a - b)^2 = c^2 - 2ab$$
$$a^2 - 2ab + b^2 = c^2 - 2ab$$
$$\text{So, } a^2 + b^2 = c^2.$$

With proofs by picture or diagram, as we see in the case of Bhaskara's visual proof, it is sometimes necessary for the prover to define the quantities labeled on the pictures and explain how to "unpack" the diagram to understand how the picture proves the theorem to be true.

The form used to represent a mathematical proof is valid when it communicates the essential features of proof, as expressed in Big Idea 2 and its associated understandings. These features are two-fold: (1) a proof must contain mathematical arguments, and (2) the arguments in a proof must be based on valid axioms, statements, or theorems. These essential elements are present even in picture proofs. In the case of Bhaskara's proof of the Pythagorean theorem, the picture itself is not the proof, but we can interpret features of the picture that can be written as a proof that does not rely on the picture. In this case, those features include the fact that it is a specifically constructed geometric object, based on assumptions such as the definition of a right triangle, Euclid's postulate that all right angles are congruent, and the fact that the angle measure of a straight line is 180 degrees.

The centrality of working with diagrams in geometry is the focus of a big idea in *Developing Essential Understanding of Geometry for Teaching Mathematics in Grades 6–8* (Sinclair, Pimm, and Skelin 2012).

Interpreting the features of a picture requires learning how to read geometric diagrams and function graphs. Consider the picture in Reflect 1.7, which can be linked to a trigonometric statement.

Reflect 1.7

What trigonometric theorem does the picture below (Osler 2002) prove?

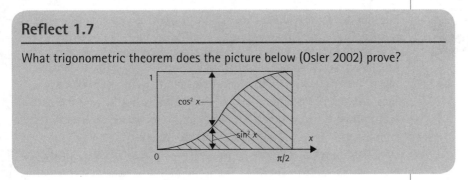

Proofs can take two-column form, pictorial form, as in Reflect 1.7, or, as in the case that follows, narrative form. In calculus, Rolle's theorem states that if $f(x)$ is continuous for $a \leq x \leq b$, $f''(x)$ exists for $a < x < b$, and $f(a) = f(b)$, then $f'(c) = 0$ for at least one value of c with $a < c < b$.

> **Proof.** Either the function is constant between a and b or it isn't. If it is constant, the derivative is 0 at each point, so we can choose any point to be the c required by the theorem. On the other hand, if the function is not constant, it must either include points above or below the common value of $y = f(a) = f(b)$. That implies that there will either be a maximum value above y, where the derivative must then equal 0, or a minimum value below y, where again the derivative must equal 0. (Larson, Hostetler, and Edwards 2002, p. 168)

Even in narrative form, the proof of Rolle's theorem relies on definitions, assumptions, and valid statements (such as the definition of a constant function) to make a deductive argument showing the truth of the theorem.

Proof Shows Truth beyond Any Doubt: Big Idea 3

Big Idea 3. *A proof demonstrates the truth of a statement beyond any doubt for all possible cases.*

The meaning of *proof* in mathematics is different from its meaning in other contexts. The methods of mathematical proof ensure that a statement has been proven beyond any doubt, as long as the definitions, theorems, and assumptions from which a proof has been constructed are valid. In professional mathematics, the process of establishing whether or not a proof is valid involves careful review by scholars—often experts in the topic of study to which the conjecture belongs—who scrutinize each statement of the proof. Once the validity of the proof has been established, the theorem can be reliably used as an assumption in proofs of new, related conjectures. In this manner, mathematical knowledge builds on a solid foundation of proven, valid theorems.

This process, while rigorous, is not infallible; in numerous instances in the history of mathematics mathematicians believed theorems to have been proven, only later to discover that the proofs were based on an incorrect assumption or contained a flaw. Experiment with the process of proof by working with the task below.

> ### Try It Yourself!
>
> Evaluate the expression $N^2 + N + 41$ for integer values of N from 1 through 5. Do you believe that this expression represents a prime number for all positive integers N? Why? (Sultan and Artzt 2010, p. 1)

After working on the task, are you convinced that the expression will always produce a prime number? How do you know for sure? As it turns out, the expression in the task above will *not* produce a prime number when $N = 41$. As you can see, evidence from empirical examples can be very convincing, but this evidence cannot prove a statement to be true for all numbers or cases. Although testing examples can be very useful for securing a better understanding of the relationships among variables in a statement, or increasing one's belief that a statement is worth trying to prove, examples are insufficient to prove a statement. To prove a statement, one must reason in a logical fashion from axioms, definitions, and statements known to be true.

A proof is only as valid as the statements, axioms, and definitions that it uses

Essential Understanding 3a. *The truth of a proved statement is dependent on the original definitions, axioms, and theorems on which the proof relies.*

Any proof is only as good as the validity of the statements on which it is based. In mathematics, axioms are statements that mathematicians have agreed can be assumed to be true, such as the statement that there exists a whole number 0. Euclid based his geometry on five postulates (axioms), and used these postulates to generate proofs for many of the theorems that he presented in his treatise, *Elements*. The five postulates of Euclidean geometry follow:

1. For any two distinct points P and Q, there is a unique line containing them.

2. Given a line segment AB and another line segment DE, we can always extend AB to AC where BC is congruent to DE.

3. For every point O and every point A not identical to O, there is a circle with center O and radius of length OA.

4. All right angles are congruent to one another.

5. From a point P outside a line l, one can draw a unique line m parallel to l (the parallel postulate).

The fifth postulate, the parallel postulate, was the most contentious of Euclid's axioms. After the time of Euclid, scores of mathematicians worked to prove the parallel postulate since this mathematical idea was thought to be complex enough to require a proof.

Gauss attempted to prove major theorems in Euclidean geometry, such as the theorem that the sum of the angle measures in a triangle equals 180 degrees, without using the parallel postulate. His work led him to discover that the sum of the angles in a triangle could be less than *or* equal to 180 degrees. Gauss was so confounded by his discovery that he was afraid to publish the results of his work. Later, a mathematician named János Bolyai defined a new, non-Euclidean geometry, *hyperbolic geometry*, which explained what Gauss had found years earlier—a geometry in which the parallel postulate did not hold.

What does this mean for proof? In Euclidean geometry, many of the proofs of theorems are based on the parallel postulate. With the development of non-Euclidean geometries, the parallel postulate could be assumed only in the realm of Euclidean geometry. A typical proof for the sum of the angle measures of a triangle is shown at the top of the next page.

Proof. Given triangle *ABC*.

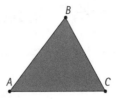

Construct a line *l* parallel to *AC* through *B*. Construct points *D* and *E* on *l* so that *B* lies between *D* and *E*.

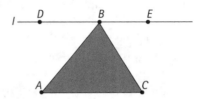

Because the angle measure of a straight line, $\angle DBE$, equals 180 degrees, $\angle DBA + \angle B + \angle EBC = 180°$. Since *l* is parallel to *AC*, $\angle DBA = \angle A$ and $\angle EBC = \angle C$ because alternate interior angles are congruent when two parallel lines are cut by a transversal. Therefore, $\angle A + \angle B + \angle C = 180°$.

The first step depends on assuming that there exists a unique line through a point outside a given line that is parallel to that given line (the parallel postulate). Gauss's discovery that if the parallel postulate were not used, the sum of the angles of a triangle could be less than 180 degrees shows how critical assumptions—and their validity—are to the proofs that we create and the knowledge that they generate.

In Euclidean geometry, where the parallel postulate is assumed, the sum of the angle measures of a triangle is 180 degrees. However, in *hyperbolic geometry*, triangles whose vertices are not collinear have angle measures whose sum is less than 180 degrees, and in *spherical geometry*, such triangles have angle measures whose sum is greater than 180 degrees. The reason that the characteristics of these non-Euclidean geometries differ so greatly from the characteristics of Euclidean geometries is that the conception of the space where points, lines, and planes exist differs markedly from the conception of space in Euclidean geometry, where lines are straight and planes are flat. For example, in spherical geometry, points are located on the sphere, and lines are the great circles formed by the slicing of the surface of the sphere by planes through the origin.

Understanding the differences between Euclidean and non-Euclidean geometries, even on a superficial level, can help us recognize how important assumptions are to how mathematical systems work and the properties of those systems. If a proof is based on faulty assumptions, either the flawed argument will suggest that a property that does not hold is true, or the assumption itself will yield a contradiction. And in the case of Euclidean geometry, not assuming certain axioms to be true can yield new mathematical discoveries!

Proof ensures that no counterexamples exist

Essential Understanding 3b. *Once a statement has been proved, finding a counterexample is not possible.*

Consider the following mathematical statement: If a and b are relatively prime integers and a divides kb for some integer k, then a must divide k. Below is a proof of this mathematical statement:

If a divides kb, then all prime factors of a divide kb. Because a and b have no prime factors in common, since they are relatively prime, all the prime factors of a divide k. Therefore, k contains all prime factors of a and is a multiple of a. So, a divides k.

The integers 180 and 1463 are relatively prime, and 180 divides the product $540 \cdot 1463$, which equals 790,020. Does 180 divide 540? If you answered yes, you are correct. How did you determine your answer? Did you do long division or use your calculator? It is pretty easy to check just by using arithmetic, but the proof above eliminates the need to check. The proof is based on general definitions of relatively prime integers and the meaning of divisibility, so the mathematical statement will hold, no matter which two relatively prime integers are considered.

The power of mathematical proof eliminates the need to verify or check whether a claim is true for specific cases. If the statements, axioms, definitions, and assumptions on which a proof relies are true, then the statement can be accepted as fact. If a counterexample were found that disproved the statement, it would mean that the argument believed to be a proof contained flaws in reasoning or had been based on false statements. The role of a mathematical *community* is crucial to the strength of a proof; having more people review and scrutinize a proof increases the likelihood that the proof is, in fact, valid. A valid proof implies the *impossibility* of counterexamples.

Not All Arguments Are Proofs: Big Idea 4

Big Idea 4. *A proof is not an argument based on authority, perception, popular consensus, intuition, probability, or examples.*

Imagine that a class of geometry students is shown the diagram in figure 1.12. Given the triangle displayed and the information that *D* and *E* are midpoints, students are asked whether segment *DE* is parallel to segment *AB*. Several students provide reasons why they think the two segments are parallel:

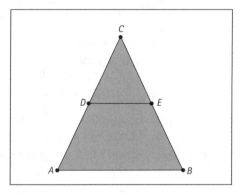

Fig. 1.12. Triangle displayed to the class

Mario: I drew a bunch of different triangles of different shapes and sizes. In every case, you can see that the segment connecting the midpoints is parallel to the base. No matter what type of triangle you draw, those segments will always be parallel.

Sue: But how do you know they are exactly parallel? Maybe they are just really close, but not exactly parallel.

Mario: It's too much of a coincidence for it to happen every time. Look, I showed it for equilateral triangles, isosceles triangles, and scalene triangles of all different shapes. If it were just close and not exact, I don't think you'd see it looking like this no matter what type of triangle I draw.

Katoya: I can show it on the board with this triangle. [*Goes up to the board.*] See, the distance between *D* and the base is [*measuring the vertical distance with a yardstick*] 7 inches. And the distance between *E* and the base is also 7 inches. So that shows that it is exactly parallel.

Ben: [*Flipping through his textbook.*] Actually, we know that it's going to be parallel if you skip ahead a little bit to section 6. Look on page 132—it has it as a theorem. It states, "The segment that joins the midpoint of two sides of a triangle is parallel to the third side." So it has to be true—it's in our book!

Teacher: So how many people think that segment *DE* is parallel to segment *AB*?

[*Everybody in the class raises a hand.*]

Teacher: It looks as though we have a consensus.

Reflect 1.8 encourages you to consider the arguments that Mario, Katoya, and Ben offer.

Reflect 1.8

Which of the arguments, if any, offered by Mario, Katoya, and Ben in the preceding dialogue do you consider appropriate for mathematical discussion?

It is common for students to decide on the truth or falsehood of a statement on the basis of reasoning that falls short of deductive proof. In this case, Mario uses a number of examples by drawing a variety of triangles. Because the midpoint segment looks parallel to the third side in each case, he decides that it must in fact be parallel. This is an example of an empirical argument, or examples-based reasoning: a student tries a number of examples and sees that the statement "works" each time. In addition, Mario relies on his perception that the line segments are parallel, even though he cannot determine this mathematically.

It might appear that Katoya's reasoning is more precise, but she also relies on perceptual judgments. She determines that the line segments for the particular triangle on the board are parallel, but she may not realize that any one particular diagram of a triangle must function as a general figure to represent all triangles. Perceptually based reasoning may be particularly common in geometry, but it can occur in any mathematics domain and may be very convincing to students.

In contrast, Ben does not rely on perception or examples, but instead finds a statement of the theorem in the textbook. Because the statement is in the book, Ben believes that it has to be true—after all, mathematics textbooks do not include false statements as theorems! Ben's belief in the truth of the statement on the basis of its appearance in the textbook is an example of authority-based reasoning (Harel and Sowder 1998). Students may also try to justify statements because they heard them from their teacher or an older sibling. If somebody with mathematical authority states that a conjecture is true, then students frequently accept this endorsement as compelling evidence of its truth. Authority-based reasoning can be convincing, particularly because students might rely on this method of justification outside of mathematics class. However, just like examples-based and perception-based reasoning, authority-based reasoning does not constitute a mathematical proof.

In addition, the teacher in this example asks the students to vote on whether they believe the statement is true, and everybody in the class is convinced. It is common practice in many mathematics classrooms to vote on whether particular ideas, approaches, or strategies make sense. Although this can at times be a powerful pedagogical technique, proof by consensus is not a valid form of mathematical proof.

Students may use many forms of reasoning to convince themselves and others of the truth of mathematical statements. Although reasoning on the basis of examples, authority, intuition, probability, or perception can at times be convincing, and can provide useful strategies for making sense of statements, such reasoning does not constitute valid mathematical proof.

Proof has special meaning in mathematics

Essential Understanding 4a. *The idea of proof in mathematics is unique and differs in notable ways from the notion of proof in science and other disciplines.*

The word *proof* is used in many different ways and in different contexts. Many children and adults have learned about the notion of proof in legal settings by watching prime-time television crime dramas. In a U.S. court of law, a defendant is innocent until proven guilty, and the prosecution is charged with the burden of proof. To discharge this burden, the prosecution must provide ample evidence (a "preponderance of evidence," in legal language), or clear and compelling evidence, as proof that the defendant is guilty of the charge of committing the crime. Mathematical proof, on the other hand, requires general arguments derived logically from accepted statements such as axioms, definitions, and theorems, rather than examples-based arguments.

People commonly hear the term *proof* in other contexts, such as a scientific context, in which results are typically regarded as *proved* when scientists can say that they are "strongly supported by scientific evidence." For instance, Newton's laws of motion provide specific predictions that can be tested empirically. One of these laws is that a mass subject to a force undergoes an acceleration that has the same direction as the force and a magnitude that is directly proportional to the force and inversely proportional to the mass. Introductory physics students learn to represent this law in the form of the equation $F = ma$. This prediction can be tested with different masses and forces, and the resulting acceleration

can be measured. Accumulating a body of evidence that repeat-
edly supports a scientific hypothesis can result in modifications
of the hypothesis, restrictions on its domain of generality, and its
general acceptance in the scientific community. People may speak
of "scientific proof," but this term refers only to a strong body of
evidence supporting a hypothesis or theory.

In mathematics, however, the notion of proof is special. As we
discussed in connection with Essential Understanding 3*b*, proof is
possible in mathematics only because mathematics is a closed discipline, founded on axioms—statements that are assumed to be true
without being proved themselves. An axiom is a self-evident assumption. For instance, one of the axioms of Euclidean geometry is
that there is one unique line that passes through two distinct points.
In constructing a proof, one relies on building blocks already accepted as true, including not only axioms but also definitions and
previously proved theorems. By building a series of deductive, logical statements based on axioms, definitions, and theorems, one can
construct a mathematical proof.

Let us return to the midpoint segment conjecture—the conjecture that the segment joining the midpoints of two sides of a triangle is parallel to the third side of the triangle. One possible proof
is the following, which draws on the diagram in figure. 1.13.

Essential ⬅
Understanding 3*b*
*Once a statement
has been proved,
finding a
counterexample is
not possible.*

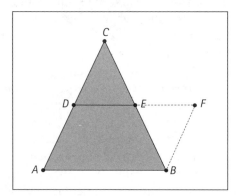

Fig. 1.13: A diagram used in proving the mid-segment conjecture

Construct segment *BF* parallel to segment *CA* and meeting line *DE* at
F. In triangles *CDE* and *BEF*, angle *C* is congruent to angle *EBF*, because segment *CA* is parallel to segment *BF*. Further, angles *CED* and
BEF are congruent because they are vertical angles, and we already
know that segment *CE* is congruent to segment *EB* because *E* is the
midpoint of the segment. Therefore, triangle *CDE* is congruent to
triangle *BFE* from the angle-side-angle theorem of triangle congruence. Hence, segment *DE* is congruent to segment *EF*, and segment
CD is congruent to segment *BF*. Because segment *CD* is congruent
to segment *AD*, since *D* is the midpoint of segment *AC*, segment *AD*
is congruent to segment *BF*. Furthermore, we constructed segment

BF to be parallel to segment *CA*, and that guarantees that *ABFD* is a parallelogram. Therefore, segment *DE* is parallel to segment *AB*.

In this case, unlike in the case of a scientific "proof" or the notion of proof in another discipline, the proof has demonstrated definitively that segment *DE must* be parallel to segment *AB*, for any possible triangle. The proof relied on basic axioms and definitions, such as the definition of a parallel line, and used previously proved theorems, such as the angle-side-angle theorem of triangle congruence. Unlike earlier arguments from Mario, Katoya, and Ben, in which the students believe the statement to be true on the basis of examples or perception, the proof provides a logical series of deductive arguments, each building on the prior statement.

Examples as a part of proving

Essential Understanding 4b. *Examples can be a critical part of the proving process but do not suffice as a mathematical proof, except in the case of proof by exhaustion or proof by counterexample.*

Working with specific examples can be very helpful for understanding the nature of a problem or for convincing oneself of the truth of a statement. Reasoning with examples is a natural and important part of mathematical reasoning and can support students' proof practices as they engage with new problems. In this section, we will discuss three different arguments in which working with examples plays an important role. In the first case, we examine the work of a student who studies multiple examples and begins to make connections and generalizations as a result of her explorations. In the second case, we discuss the idea of a proof by exhaustion by considering the conjecture that there are only two 3-digit numbers that are the sums of the cubes of their digits. In the third case, we discuss the idea of a proof by counterexample in connection with the conjecture, "If *p* is a prime number, then $2^p - 1$ must also be prime." In each case, examples play a different but critical role in supporting the development of a proof.

The first argument is the work of a student, Ella, in response to the Maximum Area problem, shown in Reflect 1.9. The solutions to this problem help to illustrate a point about the use of examples in the proving process.

Reflect 1.9

Maximum Area Problem

When will a rectangle with a fixed perimeter have the greatest area? How do you know?

Students may work with many different examples to get a sense of what is involved in the problem. Ella picks a fixed perimeter of 20 units and investigates which rectangle has the greatest area. Examples that she considers appear in figure 1.14.

Ella notices that in the case of a fixed perimeter of 20 units, the rectangle with the greatest area appears to be a square. But will that always be the case? To test this hypothesis, Ella tries several more examples, using fixed perimeters of 24 units, 40 units, 8 units, and 10 units. In trying these examples, Ella notices several things. First, a square always yields the largest area. Second, it is easiest to do calculations when the perimeter is a multiple of 4, but even in the case of a fixed perimeter of 10 units, the maximum area is 6.25 square units when all the side lengths are 2.5 units.

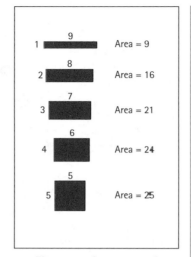

Fig. 1.14. Sequence of rectangles and their areas

This example causes Ella to wonder if she is missing any other possibilities by not considering more precise decimals. She goes back and revisits all of the other fixed perimeters, and notices that, even when she is working with decimal values, the square still yields the maximum area. For instance, with the fixed perimeter of 20 units, a rectangle that is 5.01 units by 4.99 units has an area of 24.9999 square units, still less than the maximum area of 25 square units.

The third thing that Ella notices is that as the rectangle becomes more and more nearly square, the rate at which the area changes seems to slow down. The difference between the areas of the 1×9 rectangle and the 2×8 rectangle is fairly large, 7 square units, but the difference between the areas of the 4×6 rectangle and the 5×5 rectangle is only 1 square unit. Ella observes that this pattern of change in the area is present in every example that she picks, and it reminds her of the graph of a parabola, in which the curve seems to "flatten out" close to the vertex. This prompts Ella to wonder whether she can write an expression for a functional relationship that will describe the areas of the rectangles with a fixed perimeter.

Starting with the specific example in which the perimeter was 20 units, Ella writes the equations $20 = 2l + 2w$ and $A = lw$. Substituting $10 - l$ for w, she rewrites the second equation as $A = l(10 - l)$, or $A = 10l - l^2$. She then graphs the function, as shown in figure 1.15.

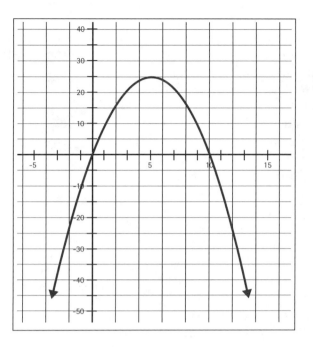

Fig. 1.15. Graph of $A = 10l - l^2$

Ella knows that that her graph is a parabola, and she sees that the vertex of the parabola is at the point (5, 25). Moreover, she is confident that she can prove that for this case the maximum area is 25 square units by determining the A-value of the vertex. Ella knows that parabolas are symmetric, and she also knows that the l-value of the vertex for this parabola is the midpoint of the two l-intercepts, (0, 0) and (10, 0). The midpoint is at $l = 5$, and therefore the A-value of the vertex is $A = 10(5) - (5)^2$, or 25.

Ella is now confident that the rectangle with the maximum area for a fixed perimeter of 20 units is a square, but how can she show that a square is the rectangle with the maximum area for *any* fixed perimeter? Extending her reasoning from the 20-unit perimeter, she can write a general equation for the area, $A = l(P/2 - l)$, for a fixed perimeter P. Multiplying through, she can then express this as $A = Pl/2 - l^2$. If she is familiar with the technique of completing the square, she can use this strategy to rewrite the equation as $A = \left(l - \dfrac{P}{4}\right)^2 + \dfrac{P^2}{16}$, which will yield the vertex $\left(\dfrac{P}{4}, \dfrac{P^2}{16}\right)$. A student who knows calculus will know, alternatively, that the function has a stationary point (a maximum, minimum, or point of inflection) when the first derivative is 0. Taking the derivative of A with respect to l, one will get $A' = P/2 - 2l$, and setting this equal to zero and solving for l will yield $l = P/4$. The function has a stationary point when the side length of the rectangle is 1/4 of the rectangle's perimeter, which will make it a square. Furthermore, the second derivative of A with respect to l is -2, which shows that the derivative function values shift from positive to negative, and therefore the stationary point is a maximum.

Not all students have access to the type of reasoning demonstrated above, but the scenario shows how a student can think about specific examples in ways that reveal a pattern, highlight some interesting relationships, and spark some ideas for moving forward. Notice that even though Ella finds, in each example she chooses, that the maximum area occurs when the rectangle is a square, she knows that this experimental result does not constitute a mathematically appropriate proof. Instead, she has to find a way to create a general relationship and prove that for any possible fixed perimeter P, the maximum area will always occur when a rectangle is a square.

In addition to helping a student develop ideas toward a possible proof, examples play important parts in proofs by exhaustion and proofs by counterexample. For instance, consider the conjecture that there are only two 3-digit numbers that are sums of the cubes of their digits. It would be possible to write a computer program to check whether this is the case for every 3-digit number. Checking 100 would show that $1^3 + 0^3 + 0^3 \neq 100$. Checking 101 would show that $1^3 + 0^3 + 1^3 \neq 101$, and so forth. Continuing this process for every 3-digit number would show that there are two numbers that satisfy the property—namely 153 and 407:

$$153 = 1^3 + 5^3 + 3^3$$
$$407 = 4^3 + 0^3 + 7^3$$

Once the program had demonstrated that no other number from 100 through 999 would satisfy this property, the proof would be complete.

In general, examples can be a very important way to refute a conjecture, check specific cases, develop a better understanding of the conjecture, and spark possible ideas for proving it. However, it is important to help students understand that verifying by examples, while often very convincing, is not sufficient as mathematical proof.

The other type of proof that relies on examples in a particular way is proof by counterexample. For instance, consider the following conjecture: "If p is a prime number, then $2^p - 1$ must also be prime." Checking the first few prime numbers, 2, 3, 5, and 7, would yield 3, 7, 31, and 127, respectively, which are indeed all prime. Proof by exhaustion is impossible for this conjecture, because there are infinitely many primes. However, in continuing to check examples, checking the prime number 11 shows that $2^{11} - 1 = 2047$. Twenty-three divides 2047 evenly, so 2047 is not prime. The existence of just one counterexample is sufficient to refute the conjecture.

For an extended study of quadratic functions, see *Developing Essential Understanding of Expressions, Equations, and Functions for Teaching Mathematics in Grades 6–8* (Lloyd, Herbel-Eisenmann, and Star 2011).

Some students may not understand the role that a counterexample plays in definitively refuting a conjecture, instead seeing a counterexample as an exception that does not generally affect the truth of the statement (Balacheff 1987). One important aspect of understanding proof is understanding that just one counterexample can refute a statement, but multiple examples are not sufficient to prove it.

The Role of Proof: Big Idea 5

Big Idea 5. *Proof has many different roles in mathematics.*

What roles does proof play in mathematics? What purposes can proof serve in developing students' mathematical understanding? What is the value of including proof in a high school mathematics class, and what roles can proof take as students learn mathematics? The five essential understandings associated with Big Idea 5 address different roles that proof can play in 9–12 mathematics. Although an exhaustive list of these roles is not possible, these essential understandings provide an overview of the roles of proof and the multiple ways in which engaging in proof and proving can enhance students' experience and understanding of mathematics.

Proof to verify the truth of a statement

Essential Understanding 5a. *One role of proof is to verify the truth or falsehood of a statement.*

In a traditional mathematics class, students may experience proof only in textbook exercises, as a mathematical technique that they are compelled to learn to demonstrate the truth of theorems already known to be true. Students know that theorems in their mathematics texts are true, even if they themselves may not fully understand them. But proof can also play a role in helping students determine whether a particular conjecture is true or false.

In this role, proof can be particularly powerful in the investigation of student-developed conjectures, but it can also play an important role in determining the truth of conjectures that are new to students. For instance, suppose that a group of beginning geometry students is investigating the question presented in Reflect 1.10 in a dynamic geometry environment.

Reflect 1.10

Exterior Angle Investigation

What is the relationship between angle 4 and the other angles in the triangle shown below? Make a conjecture yourself, and then reflect on the types of conjectures that you could imagine your students making.

The students might make a number of conjectures about angle 4. Suppose that a group of students measures all four angles and then notices that the measure of angle 4 is equal to the sum of the measures of angles 1 and 2, or $m\angle 4 = m\angle 1 + m\angle 2$. They move the triangle around in a number of different ways and find that no matter what type of triangle they have, the measure of angle 4 is always equal to the sum of the measures of angles 1 and 2. They conjecture that for any exterior angle on a triangle, the measure is equal to the sum of the measures of the two nonadjacent interior angles.

Dynamic geometry software can provide a way for students to create and test conjectures; in this case, students may be strongly convinced that their conjecture is correct because of the large number of different triangles that they are able to test. However, the role of proof in such a situation can be as a *verification* of the truth (or falsehood) of the conjecture. In this case, one simple proof relies on the fact that the sum of the measures of the angles in a triangle is 180°, and the angle measure of a straight line is 180°. Therefore, $m\angle 1 + m\angle 2 + m\angle 3 = 180°$, and $m\angle 3 + m\angle 4 = 180°$. So, $m\angle 4 = 180° - m\angle 3$, which is equivalent to $m\angle 1 + m\angle 2$. This proof has verified that the conjecture will be true for any exterior angle of any triangle.

Conviction and verification are not the same thing. For instance, one may be very convinced of the truth of a conjecture as a result of trying many different examples or viewing multiple cases by dragging a figure around in a dynamic geometry environment. However, being convinced of a statement's truth is different from verifying its truth through mathematical proof. Proof serves as a way to verify the truth of a statement definitively for every possible case.

Proof as a source of insight

Essential Understanding 5b. *Proof can provide insight into why a statement is true.*

Some proofs may simply serve to verify the truth of a statement without helping students understand why the statement is true. Researchers have referred to this as the distinction between "proofs that prove" and "proofs that explain" (Hanna 1983). Not all proofs necessarily provide insight into why a statement is true or false, but there are times when engaging in proving, or reading a proof, can help one see why the statement holds. In our discussion of Essential Understanding 2b, we presented two proofs, a written argument and a pictorial argument, to show that

$$1 + 2 + 3 + \ldots + n = \frac{n(n+1)}{2}.$$

Below we present another written argument, based on inductive reasoning.

Proof by induction. First let's check that the statement

$$1 + 2 + 3 + \ldots + n = \frac{n(n+1)}{2} \text{ is true for } n = 1: \frac{1(1+1)}{2} = \frac{2}{2} = 1$$

Now, we shall assume that the statement is true for n and show that it is true for $n + 1$:

$$1 + 2 + 3 + \ldots + n = \frac{n(n+1)}{2}$$

$$\therefore 1 + 2 + 3 + \ldots + n + (n+1) = \frac{n(n+1)}{2} + (n+1)$$

$$= \frac{n^2}{2} + \frac{n}{2} + \frac{2n}{2} + \frac{2}{2}$$

$$= \frac{n^2 + 2n + 1}{2} + \frac{n+1}{2}$$

$$= \frac{n^2 + 3n + 2}{2}$$

$$= \frac{(n+1)(n+2)}{2}$$

This proof has demonstrated that the conjecture is true for all natural numbers. It verifies *that* the conjecture is true, but does little to explain *why* it is true. For instance, students may wonder why there is a 1/2 in the original statement. For contrast, let's revisit the pictorial proof from our earlier discussion, shown on the next page as figure 1.16. Let's now supply a slightly expanded explanation.

The sum $1 + 2 + 3 + \ldots + n$ can be visualized as the first olive-colored unit square in the top left corner, plus the next two olive squares below it, plus the three below those, and so on, until we get to the n olive squares in the bottom row. One way to think about this is to imagine that the rectangle has two sets of $(1 + 2 + 3 + \ldots + n)$ squares: one set is olive, and the other set is white. Half of the area of the square is represented by the olive squares and is a set of $(1 + 2 + 3 + \ldots + n)$ unit squares. The area of the whole rectangle is $n(n + 1)$ square units. So the olive squares can be represented by $\frac{n(n+1)}{2}$.

This proof provides an explanation of why the sum can be written as $\frac{n(n+1)}{2}$ and clarifies why the conjecture contains the term 1/2. Unlike the proof by induction, it provides a rationale for understanding why it is possible to express the sum of the first n

Essential Understanding 2b *Many modes of argumentation are valid for engaging in proving and disproving statements, including deductive processes such as mathematical induction, as well as finding counterexamples.*

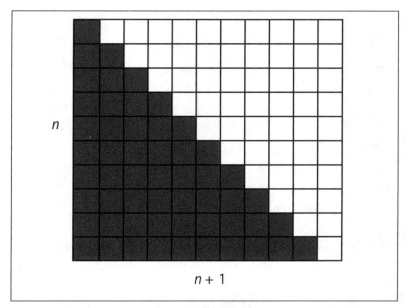

Fig. 1.16. Pictorial proof showing the sum of the first n
natural numbers

terms this way. The act of interpreting and making sense of a proof
that explains can provide insight into why a statement is true;
moreover, the act of producing a proof can also play this role.
Students can engage in proving as a way to understand why a particular conjecture must be true, so students' abilities both to produce
and to comprehend proofs can play important roles in supporting
their understanding of mathematical concepts.

Proof as an entry point

Essential Understanding 5c. *Proofs can provide an entry point for the
development of a new theory or idea.*

Imagine a group of advanced precalculus students working with a
computer graphics program to graph sin(x) and cos(x) on the same
set of axes, as in figure 1.17. Suppose that the students know that

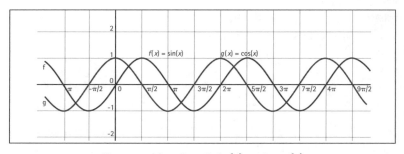

Fig. 1.17. Graphs of sin(x) and cos(x)

sine is a periodic function with a period of 2π, and they notice that the graph of $\cos(x)$ coincides with the graph of $\sin(x)$ with a horizontal translation of $\pi/2$ units: therefore, it appears that

$$\cos\left(\frac{\pi}{2} - x\right) = \sin(x).$$

The students decide to try to create a proof for this property by using the unit circle. After working for a day with some guidance from their teacher, the group creates the diagrams in figure 1.18. One student, Tessa, explains the group's reasoning:

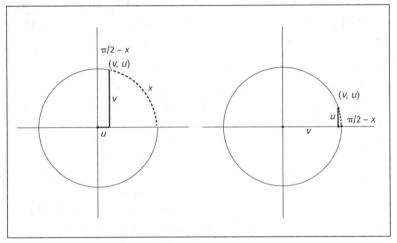

Fig. 1.18. Unit circle diagrams

The first picture shows an arc x with an endpoint (u, v), so $\sin(x) = v$. The complement of x is going to be $\left(\frac{\pi}{2} - x\right)$. So then shift the arc $\pi/2 - x$ around so that it is in standard position, as you see in the second picture. Now the endpoint is going to be (v, u), so $\cos\left(\frac{\pi}{2} - x\right) = v$. Since we already know that $v = \sin(x)$, that means that $\cos\left(\frac{\pi}{2} - x\right) = \sin(x)$.

Once the class understands the proof that Tessa's group created, they are then able to use the same unit circle and reasoning to develop the fact that $\sin\left(\frac{\pi}{2} - x\right) = \cos(x)$, as well as the cofunction properties for tangent and secant. In addition, they can continue on to develop other properties, such as the composite argument properties for $\cos(A - B)$, $\cos(A + B)$, $\sin(A - B)$, and $\sin(A + B)$.

Engaging in proof activity can provide new insights and create supports for students to explore new connections (such as that between Cartesian graphs of trigonometric functions and unit-circle representations), to articulate newly noticed relationships, or to examine ideas in a new direction. Through proving, students have opportunities to learn mathematics that is new to them. Proofs can also offer students a vehicle for understanding a new content domain in mathematics; for instance, making sense of existing proofs can support students' abilities to learn new mathematics content. This may occur when students examine proofs that their peers have created, as illustrated in the scenario presented above, or it can occur through an examination of a proof presented by a textbook or a teacher.

Proof as a structure for communication

Essential Understanding 5d. *Proofs create an appropriate structure for communicating mathematical knowledge.*

One role of proof is to convince others of the truth or falsehood of a statement in a particular community. Hanna, Jahnke, and Pulte (2009) noted that presenting and publishing proofs are the primary ways in which mathematicians communicate with one another. Proofs can reveal the habits of mind, tools, strategies, and resources used by those who created them. Who the members of the community are matters, however. What would be acceptable as a proof in a sixth-grade classroom will differ from what is acceptable in a twelfth-grade classroom, where in turn the standards will differ from those for publishing a proof in a professional mathematics journal.

Diagrams, like proofs, have histories, as discussed in *Developing Essential Understanding of Geometry for Teaching Mathematics in Grades 9–12* (Sinclair, Pimm, and Skelin 2012).

As an example of proof as communication, consider the following scenario involving a second-year algebra class. To warm up at the beginning of class, the students are working on a problem called "Condo Challenge" (adapted from Lawrence and Hennessy [2002]; Felton's [2007] study of teachers' reasoning about this problem provided the idea for the following discussion). After sharing diagrams with the students for the first four stages of a condominium development (see fig. 1.19), the teacher says, "Assuming the pattern continues, how could you come up with a way to describe the nth stage and justify that your formula is correct?"

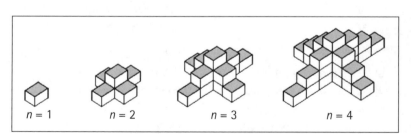

$n = 1$ $n = 2$ $n = 3$ $n = 4$

Fig. 1.19. Diagrams used in the Condo Challenge problem

One group of students makes a table of ordered pairs to represent the number of the stage, n, and the number of blocks, B, for the first four stages:

n	B
1	1
2	6
3	15
4	28

They explain, "We figured out that to get the total number of blocks, take the stage number, n, square it, multiply it by 2, and then subtract n. So for $n = 4$, you get 16 times 2 minus 4 is 28." The teacher initiates a class discussion about whether this explanation provides an acceptable justification:

Teacher: So how can you prove that this formula you developed will always work?

Elise: Well, it works for every case in the table. We tried it for $n = 1, 2, 3,$ and 4.

Teacher: I'm still not convinced that this means it will always work.

Juan: One thing we realized is that this won't be a linear function. Because if you look at the differences down the B-column, it's plus 5, then plus 9, then plus 13. So it's not adding the same amount each time, so we know it's not linear. Also, if you take the second differences, you get +4 each time. That means that it is a quadratic function, and the formula we came up with is quadratic.

Teacher: What do the rest of you think?

Sara: I agree with Juan that it has to be quadratic. And if the formula they came up with works for $n = 1, 2, 3, 4$, then it'll probably always work.

Tim: But we can't know for sure that it'll always work.

Teacher: I noticed that your method didn't make use of the diagram at all. I wonder if you could use the diagram to show that it should always work?

Juan's assertion that the function must be quadratic is true, of course, only if the function is a polynomial function. Notice that instead of addressing that issue, for which the reasoning most likely is beyond the students' current knowledge, the teacher chooses to encourage the students to think about the relationship to the diagram. At this point, the students return to their groups, and another group comes up with the following formula, which the students present on the board:

# of blocks = $n + 4$(# of blocks in the wings)

One of the students, Anna, explains:

Each stage has a tower that is n blocks tall, plus 4 wings. So we just have to figure out how many blocks are in each wing. We could do this recursively, like $1 + 2 + 3 + \ldots + n - 1$, but it's hard to represent it more directly.

This idea leads to more ways to try to figure out the number of blocks in each wing, and another group puts the following formula on the board:

$$\text{\# of blocks} = 2(n(n-1))+n$$

A member of the group, Jesse, explains how he came up with this formula by drawing a picture like that shown in figure 1.20:

Think of the stage 4 condo project. The gray blocks are one of the wings. If you turn another wing upside down and match it up, then you have this rectangle, which is 4×3, or n by $(n - 1)$. So that represents two of the wings, but since there are 4 wings total, that is $2(n)(n - 1)$. Plus the center column, like Anna said, so that's $+ n$. And this will work for any stage, because each stage has a center column n blocks high, plus 4 wings, which is always going to be of the same shape, $1 + 2 + 3 + \ldots + n - 1$.

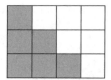

Fig. 1.20. Jesse's picture

Juan says, "This proves that our formula is correct, because if you simplify what Jesse wrote, then it's the same as our formula, $2n^2 - n$." Another student, Tara, then offers a different approach:

I have another way to prove that Juan's formula is correct. You can just solve a system of equations. Since it's a quadratic formula, you know that it will be in the form $y = ax^2 + bx + c$. So put in three points from the table and solve for a, b, and c on your calculator. That gives you $a = 2$, $b = -1$, and $c = 0$, which gives the same formula that Juan's group had.

Each group's communication of the students' proof attempts leads other students to build on their ideas to create a more robust proof. The teacher recognizes that Elise's initial explanation might be adequate in a younger group of students, but in an algebra class, her examples-based reasoning is not sufficient to demonstrate that the formula always holds. Juan's contribution adds new information, which is that they know that the formula will be quadratic. Later, Tara is able to build on Juan's thinking to prove that their formula is indeed correct by solving a system of equations. Meanwhile, Anna's explanation helps Jesse's group come up with a complete formula and rationale for why it always holds, and then connect it back to Elise and Juan's initial formula. In each case, the students' proof attempts and their descriptions help other students see the problem in new ways and develop new connections.

This example shows students communicating verbally and through pictures and formulas on the board, but written proofs can also communicate mathematical knowledge. Through the act of communicating a proof, one can convey new mathematical ideas and connections, as well as simply attempt to convince other members of a particular finding. In this sense, proof can serve not only as a confirmatory action or an action to gain a better understanding of why a theorem is true or a property holds, but also as a mode of communication. Moreover, this is a mode of communication that is particularly important in mathematical discourse, and engaging in proof as communication can enable one to become more adept at mathematical reasoning.

Proof as an impetus for precise language

Essential Understanding 5e. *Proofs provide an impetus for the use of precise mathematical language.*

One reason for introducing particular syntactic rules for proof writing is so that others can follow a proof more easily when reading it. These rules of course vary from classroom to classroom and can be influenced by many factors. For instance, Sekiguchi (2002) discusses the cultural influences on proof style, contrasting the type of proof that is typical in a U.S. high school geometry classroom with the very different format of the same proof that is more common in a Japanese classroom. Each style has its own set of advantages and drawbacks, as can be seen when comparing two proofs of the statement that if two angles of a triangle are congruent, then the sides opposite those angles are congruent. Sekiguchi illustrates the advantages and drawbacks by presenting the proofs shown in figures 1.21 and 1.22. Consider first the proof in the typical U.S. style shown in figure 1.21, which Sekiguchi draws from Jurgensen, Brown, and Jurgensen (1988).

The traditional two-column proof has a number of advantages. The format encourages explicit communication of one's reasoning in that each statement must be accompanied by a corresponding justification. The form of the justifications in the "reasons" column follows a prescribed language, so a familiarity with the relevant definitions, postulates, and theorems allows the reader to easily recognize the validity of the justification for each statement. In addition, this highly structured format can provide support to students who are learning to use precise language and rigorous reasoning

If two angles of a triangle are congruent, then the sides opposite those angles are congruent.

Given: $\angle B \cong \angle C$
Prove: $\overline{AB} \cong \overline{AC}$ [a diagram of a triangle ABC]

Proof:

Statements	Reasons
1. Draw the bisector of $\angle A$, intersecting $\overline{BC}$ at D	1. By the Protractor Postulate, an angle has exactly one bisector.
2. $\angle BAD \cong \angle CAD$	2. Def. of angle bisector
3. $\angle B \cong \angle C$	3. Given
4. $\angle BDA \cong \angle CDA$	4. If two $\angle$s of one $\triangle$ are $\cong$ to two $\angle$s of another $\triangle$, then the third $\angle$s are $\cong$.
5. $\overline{AD} \cong \overline{AD}$	5. Reflexive Property
6. $\triangle BAD \cong \triangle CAD$	6. ASA Postulate
7. $\overline{AB} = \overline{AC}$	7. Corresponding parts of $\cong \triangle$s are $\cong$.

Fig. 1.21. U.S. textbook version of two-column proof. From Sekiguchi (2002); originally in Jurgensen, Brown, and Jurgensen (1988, p. 125).

when creating deductive arguments. Examining the proof can help students become accustomed to justifying each statement in a chain of deductive reasoning.

Alternatively, the same proof can be presented in a paragraph form in a manner that is less structured than the two-column format. A proof in this style is more common in Japanese classrooms. Consider the proof in figure 1.22, which Sekiguchi (2002) draws from a Japanese textbook. In a proof of this style, a reason is not necessarily supplied for every statement, and the proof does not rely on standardized versions of definitions, postulates, and theorems. Although the proof is logically consistent, beginning students may have more difficulty in making sense of the logical flow of the statements and their justifications.

There is no one correct format for a proof. Two-column proofs are typical in geometry classrooms, but paragraph-style proofs are just as appropriate and may often represent a more meaningful way to communicate a proof. The form of a proof may evolve over the process of proving. Recall the students' activity on the Condo Challenge problem, in which they build on one another's reasoning to determine that the number of blocks can be represented by

[In △ABC, if ∠B = ∠C. then AB = AC]

[Proof] Draw the bisector of ∠A. Let its intersection with BC be D.

In △ABD and △ACD,

$$\angle B = \angle C$$

$$\angle BAD = \angle CAD \dots \text{①}$$

Because the sum of the interior angles of a triangle is 180°, the rest of the angles are equal.

$$\angle ADB = \angle ADC \dots \text{②}$$

$$AD \text{ is common} \dots \text{③}$$

Because, from ①, ②, and ③, one side and the angles at its both ends in each triangle are equal to the corresponding parts of the other, respectively,

$$\triangle ABD \equiv \triangle ACD$$

$$\text{Therefore, } AB = AC$$

Fig. 1.22. Japanese textbook version of two-column proof. From Sekiguchi (2002); originally in Tokyo Shoseki (1997, p. 118).

$2(n(n - 1)) + n$, or $2n^2 - n$. The simplicity of the formula evolves over the course of the discussion.

Moreover, Tara's proof, which comes at the end of the conversation and relies on solving a system of equations of the form $y = ax^2 + bx + c$, probably would not have occurred without the messier work of figuring out the formula to begin with. If Tara produced a final written proof based on solving a system of equations, it would probably look very different from the description that Jesse provides, relying on the picture of condo development at stage 4. Even though Jesse's explanation is just as valid as Tara's, it differs in both form and formality.

Regardless of the format of a proof, however, proof can provide a vehicle for adhering to precise and rigorous mathematical language. This can then provide students with valuable opportunities for becoming more comfortable with and adept at working toward mathematical precision.

Conclusion

Proof and proving involve processes such as conjecturing, generalizing, working with examples to develop a broader understanding, and determining the validity of existing arguments. As we have discussed in our presentation of the big ideas and the essential understandings, there are many forms of valid proofs, and proof activities can be fostered in many different ways. Proofs can exhibit varying levels of sophistication and formality, and they may occur as verbal or written arguments, pictures, algebraic expressions, or narrative

See *Developing Essential Understanding of Statistics for Teaching Mathematics in Grades 9–12* (Peck, Gould, and Miller, forthcoming) for an extensive discussion of statistical reasoning.

descriptions. The essential component of proof resides not in its form but in its function as a sequence of deductive, logical statements building from definitions, axioms, and theorems. The process of proving begins long before a student sits down to write a final argument, and it may continue far beyond the final development and refinement of a proof. These are activities that can be embedded in any mathematical content area and can become a part of regular problem solving at any grade level.

In this chapter, we have focused primarily on the definitions of proof, its various forms, and the roles that it can play in mathematics. In the next two chapters, we will discuss how proof develops across grades 9–12 and is connected to the types of justification activities that occur prior to high school as well as the more sophisticated aspects of proving that occur in more advanced mathematics. We also address the ways in which proof can be instantiated across different content areas, and we describe the challenges of teaching proof and assessing students' abilities to prove and produce proofs.

Chapter 2

Connections: Looking Back and Ahead in Learning

This chapter addresses how high school students express their understanding of proof and proving at different grade levels and in different strands of mathematics. The chapter also glances at how students' understanding of proof develops from prekindergarten to grade 8. Proof can and should be a part of 9–12 mathematics across multiple contexts, levels, and courses. Although high school geometry has traditionally been the place where proof is formally introduced into the curriculum, it can play an important role in students' learning in pre-algebra, algebra, trigonometry, precalculus, statistics, and other courses.

This chapter presents a hypothetical scenario about one problem and three different proofs that span grades and content areas of high school mathematics. On the surface, each of the proofs is about a quadratic relationship, but you will see that the proofs vary in mathematical validity, generality, and sophistication. Additionally, you will see how students can approach the same general idea from a number of different perspectives, including an algebraic perspective that is typical of students in the earlier grades in high school, a geometric perspective that is common among slightly more advanced students, and a trigonometric perspective that is characteristic of still more advanced high school students in trigonometry, precalculus, or calculus. As you read about the problem and the three proofs, think about the role that proof activities play in your own classroom and how those activities differ, depending on the age of your students and the mathematics courses in which the activities occur.

For additional discussion of the importance of generalizing, conjecturing, and justifying, see *Developing Essential Understanding of Mathematical Reasoning for Teaching Mathematics in Prekindergarten–Grade 8* (Lannin, Ellis, and Elliot 2011).

One Problem, Three Proofs

Suppose that a group of students in Ms. Tuttle's integrated math classroom is working on the Midpoint Triangle problem (a diagram appears in fig. 2.1):

Midpoint Triangle

Given an equilateral triangle *ABC*, connect the midpoints of the sides to form a second equilateral triangle, *DEF*. What is the area of triangle *DEF* compared with the area of triangle *ABC*?

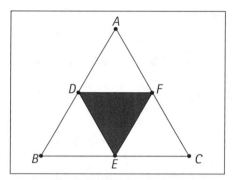

Fig. 2.1. An equilateral triangle with the midpoints forming the vertices of a second triangle

The students are able to show easily that the area of triangle *DEF* is one-fourth the area of triangle *ABC*, but then one of the students begins to wonder what would happen if the vertices of the inner triangle were not at the midpoints of the sides of triangle *ABC*:

Josh: What would the ratio be if the little triangle were not on the midpoints but instead only a third of the way?

Ella: What do you mean?

Josh: Like, right now, the points *D*, *E*, and *F* are on the midpoints. But what if they weren't on the midpoints, but instead they were a third of the way along the sides of the big triangle?

Ms. Tuttle: What would that look like?

Josh goes to the board and draws a picture to show what he means by "a third of the way." His picture shows the two triangles arranged as in figure 2.2. Josh's picture prompts some additional questions from another student, Mila:

Mila: It definitely looks like it's more than one-quarter of the area of the whole triangle. What if you kept moving the vertices so that instead of being one-third of the way, they were one-quarter of the way, or one-fifth, or really anywhere along the segments?

Ella: I think that the closer the vertices of the inside triangle get to the end, the bigger the inside triangle will be.

Ms. Tuttle: What do you mean by "the end"?

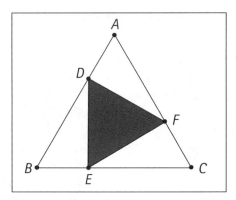

Fig. 2.2. Josh's "a third of the way" triangle

Ella: I mean, the closer the vertices of the inside triangle get to the vertices of the outside triangle, the bigger the inside triangle will get.

Ms. Tuttle: So, I have heard a number of interesting conjectures and questions. Mila has a guess that as the vertices of triangle *DEF* move closer to the points *A*, *B*, and *C*, the ratio of the area of triangle *DEF* to the area of triangle *ABC* will grow larger. This suggests a more general question: How can you compare the ratio of the areas of the two triangles, in general, as a function of the location of the vertices of triangle *DEF*? In other words, how can you compare the ratio of the area of triangle *DEF* to the area of triangle *ABC* as a function of the ratio of *AD* to *AB*?

Ms. Tuttle's question merits consideration. Reflect 2.1 focuses attention on the question and the challenges that it entails.

Reflect 2.1

Before reading further, consider Ms. Tuttle's question yourself, and see if you can determine an answer and a proof. What challenges do you face in trying to solve the problem?

Argument 1—Empirical algebraic justification

Ms. Tuttle instructs the students to return to their small groups to investigate this question and see whether they can come up with an answer and a proof. Several groups of students decide to investigate the question with dynamic geometry software. The students in one group use the program's measurement functions to create a table, shown in figure 2.3, for several different locations of the vertices of the inner triangle. They then develop the following argument:

Argument 1: The table shows us that Mila's conjecture was correct. As the vertices of triangle *DEF* move closer to the vertices of triangle *ABC*, the area grows bigger and bigger until the ratio of the area of triangle *DEF* to the area of triangle *ABC* reaches 1. Also, when the vertices are at the midpoints of triangle *ABC*, the ratio is the smallest, at $1/4$. In decimal form, the ratios look like they grow smaller until they reach a minimum at 0.25, and then larger again, so we thought the function would be a quadratic. We also know that the vertex of the parabola should be at (0.5, 0.25) because the smallest area ratio is 0.25 and that happens when the ratio of *AD* to *AB* is 0.5.

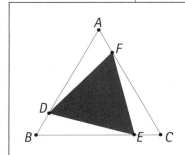

$\dfrac{AD}{AB}$	.04	.12	.22	.33	.42	.50	.63	.74	.82	.93
$\dfrac{\text{Area of } \triangle DEF}{\text{Area of } \triangle ABC}$	.88	.68	.49	.34	.27	.25	.30	.42	.56	.80

Fig. 2.3. A table comparing the ratio of the area of triangle *DEF* to the area of triangle *ABC* as a function of vertex locations

We then plotted the data from the table on our graphing calculators, and the points did look like a parabola, and we then found a curve of best fit. We chose the quadratic regression program because we knew the function should be quadratic. The program gave us the function $y = 3x^2 - 3x + 1$. Then we graphed $y = 3x^2 - 3x + 1$ on top of the points from the table, and they matched up perfectly. Also, the vertex of the parabola is at (0.5, 0.25), just as we predicted, so we knew that the function had to be correct.

Reflect 2.2 invites you to evaluate the students' argument.

Reflect 2.2

What is your opinion of the students' reasoning in argument 1? Is their argument a valid proof? What are its strengths and weaknesses?

Argument 1 might be labeled as a "proof," in quotation marks, because the students rely in part on empirical data to demonstrate the truth of their conjecture that the function relating the ratios of the areas is quadratic. For this reason, it does not adhere to the characterization of a proof in Big Idea 2. However, although argument 1 shows elements of examples-based reasoning commonly seen in arguments constructed by middle school students, it also shows signs that the students are moving beyond some elements of this type of reasoning. The students' initial supposition that the data represent a quadratic relationship appears to be based on the empirical evidence gathered in their explorations in the dynamic geometry environment and from the table that they subsequently create. Yet, the students also deduce that if 0.25 is the smallest ratio, it will have to be the y-value of the vertex of the parabola. The fact that the curve of best fit, $y = 3x^2 - 3x + 1$, matches the plotted points and yields the predicted vertex serves as confirmation for the students that the function is correct. The students therefore justify the accuracy of their solution with empirical data, but they do not demonstrate conclusively that $y = 3x^2 - 3x + 1$ must be the function that satisfies the ratio of the areas of the triangles.

The students' use of technology to determine a curve of best fit is certainly an appropriate and helpful way to think about the problem. *In Focus in High School Mathematics: Reasoning and Sense Making in Statistics and Probability*, Shaughnessy, Chance, and Kranendonk (2009) emphasize that students' statistical reasoning can be a powerful tool for fostering generalizations. However, to prove the generalized claim, students eventually must shift to deductive reasoning. Chapter 3 discusses some techniques that teachers can use to help students shift beyond arguments that rely on empirical evidence. In this case, the teacher could ask the students to think about whether it would be possible to prove that the quadratic function that they determined is the *only* function that could match their given points. One could even ask the students whether they think it would be possible to draw a different (non-polynomial) type of graph that would match each of the supplied points. Once students had determined that there could be other functions that would satisfy their set of points, they might be motivated to consider an alternative proof.

Examples-based reasoning may continue to be convincing to students at the 9–12 level, and we should expect students entering high school to operate according to this way of thinking. However, we might also see students' proofs beginning to incorporate elements of reasoning beyond the simple use of examples, in the manner of argument 1. Thinking through examples or using data to make sense of a situation can be an appropriate way to gain a better understanding of the phenomena at hand (Essential Understanding 4b). The students' investigation of the problem includes a number of powerful elements, and their understanding of quadratic functions enables them to make reasoned guesses about

See *Developing Essential Understanding of Rational Numbers for Teaching Mathematics in Grades 3–5* (Barnett-Clarke et al. 2010) or *Developing Essential Understanding of Ratios, Proportions, and Proportional Reasoning for Teaching Mathematics in Grades 6–8* (Lobato and Ellis 2010) for a discussion of how a ratio such as *AD* to *AB*, or 1 to 2, can be reinterpreted and expressed in the decimal form 0.5.

Big Idea 2

A proof is a specific type of mathematical argument, which is a connected sequence of deductive, logical statements in support of or against a mathematical claim.

Essential Understanding 4b
Examples can be a critical part of the proving process but do not suffice as a mathematical proof, except in the case of proof by exhaustion or proof by counterexample.

what type of algebraic relationship would best fit the data that they generated. With appropriate support, students at this level may be poised to move beyond examples-based arguments to construct more deductive arguments.

Argument 2—Deductive geometric justification

Students in another group construct a different type of justification that does not rely on empirical data from a table. Working with a picture like that in figure 2.4, they have already proved two things: first, that triangle *DEF* is equilateral even when its vertices are not on the midpoints of triangle *ABC*, and second, that triangles *AED*, *CFE*, and *BDF* are congruent. We pick up on their argument at the point when the students are moving on to prove the general case for comparing the ratios of the areas of the two triangles as a function of the location of the vertices of triangle *DEF*. Their argument follows:

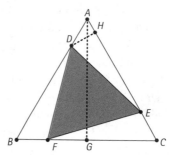

Fig. 2.4. Equilateral triangle *ABC* with inner equilateral triangle *DEF* and auxiliary segments *AG* and *DH*

Argument 2: We know that triangle *ABC* is equilateral, and it doesn't really matter how long the sides are. Let's just say that each side is 1 unit long because that is the easiest way to do it. We're also going to call the ratios *AD/AB*, *CE/CA*, and *BF/BC*, which we said are equivalent, *x*. So if each side—*AB*, *BC*, and *AC*—has a length 1, and *AD/AB*, = *CE/CA* = *BF/BC* = *x*, then that means *AD* = *BF* = *CE* = *x*. So then *BD* = *CF* = *AE* = 1 − *x*. What we need to show is how the area of triangle *DEF* compares to the area of triangle *ABC*. To do that, we can try to calculate the areas of each of those triangles.

Since each side of triangle *ABC* is 1, we can find its height, *AG*. We know that $GC = \frac{1}{2}$ and $AC = 1$, so by the Pythagorean theorem, its height is $\frac{\sqrt{3}}{2}$, so the area of triangle *ABC* is $\frac{\sqrt{3}}{4}$. But how can we find the area of triangle *DEF?* We couldn't figure out a way to do this directly, so what we did instead was find the areas of the other triangles—*AED*, *CFE*, and *BDF*—and subtract them from $\frac{\sqrt{3}}{4}$. So, for instance, with triangle *AED*, we know that its base *AE* is 1 – *x*. So, how do we figure out the height, *DH?* We used similar triangles to do this. Because *ADH* and *AGC* are both right triangles and each also has a 60° angle, we know they are similar triangles. So that means that the ratio of their sides is equal, so *AD/AC* = *DH/AG*. We know *AC* = 1, *AD* = *x*, and *AG* = $\frac{\sqrt{3}}{2}$, so *x*/1 = *DH*/($\frac{\sqrt{3}}{2}$), and solving for *DH*, we got ($\frac{\sqrt{3}}{2}$)*x*. So that means the height is ($\frac{\sqrt{3}}{2}$)*x*, and the length is 1 – *x*, so the area of triangle *AED* is ($\frac{\sqrt{3}}{4}$)(*x*)(1 – *x*). So, if we subtract three of these areas from the area of the big triangle, *ABC*, we get $\frac{\sqrt{3}}{4}$ – 3*x*($\frac{\sqrt{3}}{4}$ (1 – *x*) = ($\frac{\sqrt{3}}{4}$)(3*x*² – 3*x* + 1). That's the area of triangle *DEF*. So how does the area of triangle *DEF* compare with the area of triangle *ABC?* The ratio of triangle *DEF* to triangle *ABC* is

$$\frac{\left(\sqrt{3}\middle/4\right)\left(3x^2 - 3x + 1\right)}{\sqrt{3}\middle/4},$$

an expression that is algebraically equivalent to $3x^2 - 3x + 1$. So the ratio can be written as a quadratic expression.

Respond to Reflect 2.3 by evaluating this argument.

Reflect 2.3

What is your opinion of the students' reasoning in argument 2? Is their argument a valid proof? What are its strengths and weaknesses?

Arguments 1 and 2 compared

Arguments 1 and 2 differ in a number of ways. In producing argument 1, the students rely on empirical evidence from their table of data to conjecture that the function should be quadratic, and their justification is also partially empirical:

We graphed $y = 3x^2 - 3x + 1$ on top of the points from the table, and they matched up perfectly. Also, the vertex of the parabola is at (0.5, 0.25), just as we predicted, so we knew that the function had to be correct.

By contrast, the students producing argument 2 rely on deductive statements (Big Idea 2) to support their final claim that the function comparing the area of triangle *DEF* to that of triangle *ABC* as a function of the ratio of *AD* to *AB* is $3x^2 - 3x + 1$. Furthermore, these students rely on their existing knowledge of particular geometric definitions and theorems germane to similar triangles, right triangles, and ways of finding the areas of triangles (Essential Understanding 2a). Argument 2 is a sophisticated argument, and although many students might not produce so polished a proof, this type of proof is one that students are almost certain to see in their geometry textbooks.

Content area differences: Algebra versus geometry

An obvious difference between arguments 1 and 2 is the type of knowledge that the students rely on to build them. In constructing argument 1, the students make use of an algebraic understanding of functions and statistical reasoning about curves of best fit. They recognize the likelihood that the data represent a quadratic function from the way in which the ratio of the areas shrinks to a minimum value and then grows again, and they rely on their knowledge of quadratic functions and the graphs of these functions to deduce that the vertex is the point (0.5, 0.25). An investigation like the one that produces argument 1 is not unusual in an algebra course.

By contrast, in constructing argument 2, the students rely on their knowledge of geometry and triangle relationships to generate the series of deductions in this argument. For instance, the students rely on their understanding of a prerequisite theorem, the Pythagorean theorem, which is a salient feature of many proofs in geometry. Even though both groups of students investigate the same set of relationships, the domains of knowledge that they draw on differ. Proving activities should occur in algebra and other courses just as often as in geometry courses; there is no domain of mathematics in which proving is not an appropriate activity.

Grade–level differences

Arguments 1 and 2 differ significantly in the degree of sophistication. An argument such as argument 1 might be more prevalent among younger students in the early high school years, particularly because it exhibits a heavy reliance on empirical reasoning as well as on some unfounded assumptions. Students who still rely primarily on empirical reasoning may require explicit support to move beyond examples-based arguments to more deductive arguments. In contrast, argument 2 reveals a degree of sophistication in its logical chain of arguments and clear explanations of the sort that typically do not occur until students have had a great deal of practice in reasoning deductively and producing justifications. Argument 2 represents a more sophisticated argument than argument 1, even though both are types of arguments that are commonly constructed by high school students.

Argument 3—Trigonometric justification

Moving to an example of how proof is an appropriate activity in content areas beyond algebra and geometry, let's consider an argument by a student about a non-equilateral extension of the earlier investigations. Again, the focus is on the ratio of the areas of the original triangle and an inner triangle formed by connecting points that lie on the original triangle's sides and are in the same relationship with each of its vertices:

Non-Equilateral Extension

What if the initial triangle, *ABC*, is not equilateral? Does the same relationship hold between its area and that of an inner triangle formed by connecting points on its sides in the same way as before? If not, what is the new relationship? Or is it the case that several relationships exist, depending on the triangle? What challenges did you face when trying to solve the problem?

Suppose that the Non-Equilateral Extension problem is given to a class of trigonometry students, and one student produces the following justification:

Argument 3: Consider triangle *ABC*, as shown in the diagram [see fig. 2.5], with sides *a*, *b*, and *c*, and height *h*. The area of triangle *ABC* is $(1/2)bh$. Since *h* can also be expressed as $c(\sin A)$, the area of triangle *ABC* can be expressed as $(1/2)bc(\sin A)$; alternatively, the area of triangle *ABC* can be expressed as $(1/2)ab(\sin C)$ or $(1/2)ac(\sin B)$. Say the locations of the vertices of the inner triangle, *DEF* [see fig. 2.6], are determined by the ratio *r*, so that $(DB/AB) = (AE/AC) = (FC/BC) = r$. So, for example, if $r = 0.5$, then the vertices of triangle *DEF* are at the midpoints of their respective sides of triangle *ABC*.

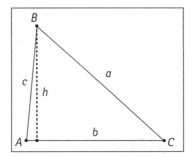

Fig. 2.5. Non-equilateral triangle *ABC* with height *h*

In the next diagram [see fig. 2.6], the lengths of the segments of each of the sides of the triangle are shown in relationship to r. So, for instance, for the side AB, because $DB/AB = r$, and the length of AB is defined as c in the diagram, then the length of DB is rc, and the length of AD is $c - rc$.

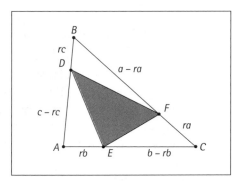

Fig. 2.6. Triangle ABC with inner triangle DEF

To find the area of triangle DEF, we can calculate it indirectly by finding the areas of triangles ADE, CEF, and BDF, and then subtracting the sum of these three areas from the area of triangle ABC. Using the triangle area formula, we can determine the area of triangle ADE to be $(\frac{1}{2})(rb)(c - rc)(\sin A)$. In a similar fashion, the area of triangle CEF and the area of triangle BDF are $(\frac{1}{2})(b - rb)(ra)(\sin C)$ and $(\frac{1}{2})(a - ra)(rc)(\sin B)$, respectively. Since the area of triangle DEF = (area of triangle ABC – area of triangle ADE – area of triangle CEF – area of triangle BDF), when we substitute the triangle area expressions, we find that the area of triangle DEF is the following:

$$\text{Area of } \triangle ABC - \frac{rb(c-rc)\sin A}{2} - \frac{ra(b-rb)\sin C}{2} - \frac{rc(a-ra)\sin B}{2}$$

$$= \text{Area of } \triangle ABC - \frac{rbc(\sin A)-r^2bc(\sin A)-rab(\sin C)+r^2ab(\sin C)-rac(\sin B)+r^2ac(\sin B)}{2}$$

$$= \text{Area of } \triangle ABC - \frac{r\big(bc(\sin A)-ab(\sin C)-ac(\sin B)\big)-r^2\big(bc(\sin A)-ab(\sin C)-ac(\sin B)\big)}{2}$$

$$= \text{Area of } \triangle ABC - \frac{(r-r^2)\big(bc(\sin A)+ab(\sin C)+ac(\sin B)\big)}{2}$$

$$= \text{Area of } \triangle ABC - \frac{(r-r^2)(6\cdot\triangle ABC)}{2}, \text{ since Area of } \triangle ABC = \frac{bc(\sin A)}{2}=\frac{ab(\sin C)}{2}=\frac{ac(\sin B)}{2}$$

Thus, Area of $\triangle DEF$ = (Area of $\triangle ABC$)$(1 - 3r + 3r^2)$.

Expressing the ratio of the areas of the triangles (area of triangle DEF/area of triangle ABC) as a function of the ratio of the sides (DB/AB), r, results in the quadratic expression $3r^2 - 3r + 1$.

Evaluate this argument, as Reflect 2.4 suggests.

Reflect 2.4

What is your opinion of the student's reasoning in argument 3? Is the argument a valid proof? What are its strengths and weaknesses?

Argument 3 relies on the student's knowledge of right triangle trigonometry, in contrast to the previous proofs, which rely on students' understanding of functional relationships in algebra and geometric theorems, respectively. As students progress through high school, the subjects of their proofs will become more sophisticated, as will the types of proofs that they produce. Beginning high school students should be able to prove that the ratio of the area of triangle DEF to the area of triangle ABC is 1/4 when the vertices of triangle DEF are the midpoints of the sides of triangle ABC. Arguments 1 and 2 tackle a more general relationship about the ratio of the areas when with the vertices of triangle DEF are not confined to the midpoints of the side of triangle ABC. Argument 3 generalizes this relationship even further by no longer requiring triangle ABC to be equilateral. Algebra and geometry students would be at a loss to prove the more general relationship in argument 3, but by the time students reach trigonometry, they have the tools to tackle this question. As students move through high school, the generality of what they are able to prove increases with the growth of their content knowledge.

Horizontal and Vertical Articulation of Proof across Strands and Grades

When we examine the three arguments presented above, we see that the first group of students make use of their understanding of algebraic functions and the meaningful connections across tables, equations, and graphs to generate their argument. The second group of students instead rely on their knowledge of geometry to produce a much more traditional geometric proof, whereas the student producing argument 3 makes use of an understanding of trigonometric relationships. The differences in the content that supports the generation of the three arguments demonstrate the important fact that proving is a critical mathematical activity in every high school mathematics class, including algebra, geometry, trigonometry, precalculus, and other courses. Generating proofs and making sense of proofs can support students' understanding in all areas of mathematics, and it is just as important to encourage this activity in algebra or trigonometry as it is in geometry.

We can think of proving as a trajectory in the learning of mathematics from prekindergarten to grade 16: the nature, content, and form of the proofs that we expect from students evolve over time. In particular, proofs may vary in *form*, in *mode of argumentation*, and in *degree of generality* as students experience repeated meaningful proof activities throughout their school careers.

Evolving forms of proof

As students progress through school mathematics, the forms of their arguments can evolve in sophistication, differ across content areas, and progress from example-based arguments to deductive proofs. Consider some examples of the more common forms of proof typical at the high school level and prior to high school:

- *Picture.* Some proofs may take the form of a picture that students use to explain a general idea. This form may be prevalent among middle school students or younger high school students who have yet to develop the algebraic facility to express relationships concisely. For instance, consider an eighth-grade student's justification, shown in figure 2.7, of the conjecture that doubling the height and length of a rectangle will quadruple its area.

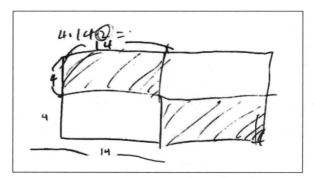

Fig. 2.7. Picture of a 4 × 14 rectangle that doubled in height and length

We worked with Daeshim, the middle school student who created this pictorial justification, in an after-school teaching session. The picture specifically represents a 4-centimeter-by-14-centimeter rectangle, yet Daeshim capitalized on the drawing in a general way to explain why the area of any rectangle will quadruple when its height and length doubles.

- *Verbal description.* Students who struggle to create narrative explanations such as those in arguments 1, 2, and 3 may be able to explain their reasoning verbally in a manner that is general and deductive. For instance, referring to the picture in figure 2.7, a student explains, "This rectangle doubled its height and doubled its length. So I can draw three extra rectangles by doing that, and you can see that there are now four equal rectangles after doubling. That means the area will be four times as big." As students progress through the grades, their abilities to represent general ideas in words and with mathematical language should increase.

- *Diagram-based arguments.* Arguments 2 and 3 rely on diagrams that the students generate to support their reasoning. Although this practice may be most prevalent in geometry, students can also use it in other content areas. For instance, our discussions of Essential Understanding 2b and Essential Understanding 5b showed students relying on diagrams to prove that

$$1 + 2 + 3 + \dots + n = \frac{n(n+1)}{2}.$$

- *Two-column proof.* The students could have used the two-column form for argument 2, as is common in geometry classes. An example of this type of proof appeared in our discussion of Essential Understanding 5e, in which we presented proofs of the statement that if two angles of a triangle are congruent, then the sides opposite those angles are congruent. The two-column proof format is still common in many geometry textbooks, and this approach may prove helpful to some students who desire extra structure to support their thinking. This form of proof might be less prevalent among students in higher grades with more experience in proving.

- *Narrative style.* All three arguments in this chapter were in a narrative, paragraph style, and relied on the students' abilities to express relationships either algebraically or with conventional geometry representations. Students often enter high school with few experiences in proving, and so they may be less comfortable with this style of argument.

- *Oral explanation.* Students can supply arguments that are not necessarily written or drawn but are spoken explanations that they give as they justify their reasoning to peers or to the classroom community. For instance, in the scenario involving the Condo Challenge problem in our discussion of Essential Understanding 5d, Jesse explains the situation to the class orally:

> Think of the stage 4 condo. The gray blocks are one of the wings. If you turn another wing upside down and match it up, then you have this rectangle, which is 4 × 3, or n by (n – 1). So that represents two of the wings, but since there are 4 wings total, that is 2(n)(n – 1). Plus the center column, like Anna said, so that's + n. And this will work for

Essential ←
Understanding 2b
Many modes of argumentation are valid for engaging in proving and disproving statements, including deductive processes such as mathematical induction, as well as finding counterexamples.

Essential ←
Understanding 5b
Proof can provide insight into why a statement is true.

Essential ←
Understanding 5e
Proofs provide an impetus for the use of precise mathematical language.

Essential ←
Understanding 5d
Proofs create an appropriate structure for communicating mathematical knowledge.

any stage, because each stage has a center column n blocks high, plus 4 wings, which is always going to be of the same shape, $1 + 2 + 3 + ... + n - 1$.

Jesse's argument was a valid proof that he explained orally.

Changing modes of argumentation

The *mode of argumentation* for a proof can also change across grade bands and content strands of mathematics. The picture in figure 2.7 can be used to support a *generic example*. Even though the rectangle is a specific rectangle rather than a general $H \times L$ rectangle, one can use it to explain a more general relationship between changing dimensions and changing area. The justification in argument 1 is, in contrast, partly dependent on examples, representing a way of thinking that uses *empirical evidence*. Although an argument based on empirical evidence is not mathematically appropriate as a proof, the prevalence of this type of argument among students—particularly younger students at the middle school level or early years in high school—makes empirical arguments important for teachers to be familiar with. Arguments 2 and 3 are more straightforward *deductive arguments*, which students in high school should be poised to generate with proper support. As students progress through high school, it may be more common for them to use other modes of argumentation, such as *proof by contradiction, proof by induction*, and *proof by exhaustion*. These modes may at times be quite sophisticated in their construction and execution. For instance, consider the proof in a precalculus course of the fact that e is irrational, which relies on the fact that e can be expressed by the infinite sum

$$e = 1 + \frac{1}{1!} + \frac{1}{2!} + \frac{1}{3!} + ... :$$

Let's multiply both sides of the above equation by $q!$

$$q!e = q! + \frac{q!}{1!} + \frac{q!}{2!} + \frac{q!}{3!} + ... + \frac{q!}{q!} + q!\left(\frac{1}{(q+1)!} + \frac{1}{(q+2)!} + \frac{1}{(q+3)!} + ... \right)$$

Since $e = \frac{p}{q}$, $q!e$ is an integer, as is the sum

$$q! + \frac{q!}{1!} + \frac{q!}{2!} + \frac{q!}{3!} + ... + \frac{q!}{q!}.$$

Thus, the sum of the remaining terms is equal to the difference of two integers. So they sum to an integer. Let's call these remaining terms R, and use the sum of the geometric series, $s = \dfrac{a(a - r^n)}{1 - r}$.

$$R = q!\left(\frac{1}{(q+1)!} + \frac{1}{(q+2)!} + \frac{1}{(q+3)!} + \cdots\right)$$

$$R = \frac{1}{(q+1)} + \frac{1}{(q+1)(q+2)} + \frac{1}{(q+1)(q+2)(q+3)} + \cdots < \frac{1}{(q+1)} + \frac{1}{(q+1)^2} + \frac{1}{(q+1)^3} + \cdots$$

$$R < \frac{1}{(q+1)}\left(1 + \frac{1}{(q+1)} + \frac{1}{(q+1)^2} + \cdots\right)$$

$$R < \frac{1}{(q+1)}\left(\frac{1}{1 - \frac{1}{(q+1)}}\right) = \frac{1}{(q+1)}\left(\frac{q+1}{q}\right)$$

$$R < \frac{1}{q}$$

Looking at our original definition of R, we see that since q is positive, so is R. Thus, R is an integer between 0 and $1/q$. This is a contradiction, so the original assumption that e is rational must be false. Therefore, e is irrational.

This type of proof relies on assuming the opposite of that which is to be proved and then arriving at a contradiction; it may be confusing for younger high school students, but, like proof by induction, this mode of argumentation is not uncommon in precalculus and calculus textbooks.

Advancing levels of generality

The sophistication of students' proofs evolves across grade bands as students' arguments progress not only in form and in type, but also in degree of generality. We see this growth in sophistication in the the arguments related to the triangle problem as students become able to address more general relationships. As students gain more experience in creating and proving conjectures, the breadth of what they are able to prove expands. Although students may enter high school with a strong orientation toward specific problems, concrete representations, and examples-based arguments, having had regular and in-depth experiences in proof and proving at every grade level can aid their development of sophistication in proving throughout high school.

Conclusion

This chapter has discussed ways in which students' skill in constructing mathematical arguments grows as their knowledge of mathematical content develops and expands, giving them a wider and richer variety of tools on which to draw when they probe, test, and refine conjectures. As students learn more mathematics, their arguments evolve, becoming more varied and sophisticated in form and mode of argumentation and increasing in degree of generality. In the next chapter, we will consider the challenges of supporting high school students and assessing their progress as they learn how to investigate and justify assertions in mathematics.

Chapter 3

Challenges: Learning, Teaching, and Assessing

To many, *proof* is a bad word in school mathematics. Many adults, including some math teachers, remember feeling confused and frustrated—even stupid—the first time that they wrote a proof in high school geometry because doing a proof seemed so difficult. Unlike much of what students learn in school mathematics, proving is a complex process that cannot be completed by using a formula or applying a procedure. Mathematicians who have successfully proven many theorems and conjectures often struggle to write a proof of a new theorem, and they sometimes do not complete a proof for months, years, or even decades. It is not surprising that students often find proving difficult, and the prevalence of this experience makes it even more important that students have many opportunities to learn how to understand, evaluate, and generate proofs throughout the school mathematics curriculum.

This chapter outlines three key learning goals to guide the planning and teaching of lessons that support students' abilities to understand, evaluate, and generate mathematical proof. These goals are intended to help students accomplish the following:

1. Develop fluency in proving

2. Understand the limitations of examples

3. Move beyond examples-based arguments to deductive proofs

The big ideas and essential understandings presented in chapter 1 lay a conceptual foundation to guide the planning and teaching of lessons aimed at achieving these goals. The goals are not specific to particular mathematical content or grade levels, nor do they represent an exhaustive list of goals to consider in teaching proof. Rather, they represent fundamental aspects of learning to prove, taking into consideration common difficulties that students have and misconceptions that they develop when proving in school mathematics. The goals are interrelated, and they can be regarded as objectives for helping students understand mathematics in a meaningful way. To help in achieving the learning goals in the classroom, the chapter offers tips on—

- using productive teaching moves;
- designing problems and activities; and
- building a classroom culture.

A later section in the chapter offers tips on assessing students' progress toward the learning goals. Planning, teaching, and assessing with these learning goals in mind can lead to more meaningful opportunities for students to engage in proving.

Learning Goal 1: Developing Fluency in Proving

Every time a student presents a conjecture in the classroom is an opportunity to engage students in proving. Classroom scenarios offer examples of common issues that arise when students attempt to prove their reasoning, and examination of these scenarios can suggest particular instructional moves that support students' work without eliminating the challenge of proving that is productive for learning.

The following excerpt showcases dialogue between a teacher and students about the formula for the sum of an infinite convergent geometric series. Before the episode captured in the scenario, the class explored how dividing a line segment of arbitrary length AB in half creates two segments of length $1/2\,AB$, and then dividing those two segments in half again yields four segments of length $1/4\,AB$, and so on. The result of the exploration was the sequence AB, $1/2\,AB$, $1/4\,AB$, $1/8\,AB$, ... to describe the lengths of the parts of the segment, and the class agreed that the sequence is infinite. In what follows, the teacher probes their intuition about the sum of this infinite sequence:

Teacher: OK, so we assume that this sequence [*points to the sequence on the board*] goes on for infinity. What is the sum of the values in this sequence? If you were to add up $1 + 1/2 + 1/4 + 1/8$, and so on, for infinity, what would we get?

Todd: We couldn't actually add them all up—it's impossible to do since it goes on for infinity.

Teacher: This is very true.

Rianne: I bet the sum is zero!

Teacher: OK, so Todd and Rianne think that either we can't find the sum, or the sum is zero. Let's start small. Let's make a table of what we call the *partial sums*—start by computing the sum for just $1 + \frac{1}{2}$. Just the sum of the first two terms. Then find the sum for the first three terms. On one side of your table, keep track of how many terms you are adding together. On the other side of your table, keep track of the sums. Do this until you have found the sum of the first five terms. Then what I want you to do is look at the sums, and write down any patterns or anything else that you notice.

The class works for about ten minutes to complete their tables of partial sums. The teacher calls on Kelly to share her observations:

Kelly: I notice that the sums are fractions, and they keep increasing by smaller and smaller amounts.

Matt: Yeah—kind of like the values in the sequence. It seems like if we keep going we might get close to 2, but I'm not sure if we would ever get to 2.

Teacher: So, Matt is suggesting that if we add up all of the terms in the sequence 1, $\frac{1}{2}$, $\frac{1}{4}$, $\frac{1}{8}$, ..., an infinite sequence, we'll get some number—maybe 2. Is there any way we could find the sum for the first two hundred values of the sequence?

Todd: Well, I looked in our book and saw that there is a formula for finding the sum of n terms of an infinite sequence like 1, $\frac{1}{2}$, $\frac{1}{4}$, ... It says that the formula is $(a - ar^n)/(1 - r)$. I have no idea what a and r are, though.

Teacher: [*Writing the formula on the board*] You're right, Todd, that the formula you read can be used to find the sum of the first 200 terms of our sequence. But we need to understand why the formula works before we can use it—and we certainly need to know what a and r are! So, a is your starting term in the sequence—it is what you multiply or divide a number by to get the next term in the sequence. The letter r stands for the common ratio that describes the difference between each term and the next in the sequence. So, for the sum of our sequence, $1 + \frac{1}{2} + \frac{1}{4}$, and so forth, our starting term, a, is 1, and our r is $\frac{1}{2}$ because we divided each term in the sequence by 2, which is equivalent to multiplying by $\frac{1}{2}$. So, another way of writing the sum of our sequence is $1 + 1 \cdot \frac{1}{2} + 1 \cdot \frac{1}{2} \cdot \frac{1}{2} + 1 \cdot \frac{1}{2} \cdot \frac{1}{2} + ...$, or, using a's and r's, $a + a \cdot r + a \cdot r \cdot r + a \cdot r \cdot r \cdot r + ...$.

Kelly: So the sum of the sequence is just 1 divided by 1 minus $\frac{1}{2}$, which is the same as $\frac{1}{2}$. One divided by $\frac{1}{2}$ is... 2! It is 2!

Teacher: So, here's what is important. Although the book tells us that this is the formula, we shouldn't use it until we have proved that it is correct. So, before you can use Todd's formula to find the sum of $1 + \frac{1}{2} + \frac{1}{4} + \ldots$, you have to show me why $a + a \cdot r + a \cdot r^2 + a \cdot r^3 + \ldots + a \cdot r^{199} = (a - ar^{200})/(1 - r)$.

Looking around the class, the teacher sees that most of the students appear to be bewildered. They are stuck. Consider the alternative representation presented in Reflect 3.1.

Reflect 3.1

Below is a representation of the infinite geometric series
$$1 + \frac{1}{2} + \frac{1}{4} + \ldots$$

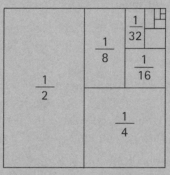

Does the picture prove that the sum is 2? What connections can you make between the representation and the formula for the sum of an infinite geometric series?

Can you construct another valid representation of the infinite geometric series $1 + \frac{1}{2} + \frac{1}{4} + \ldots$? Ask your students, and see what pictures they create.

Introducing proof outlines

Teaching Moves Tip 1

Use proof outlines as instructional tools.

From a teacher's point of view, moments when students are stuck present some of the most challenging classroom situations. We want students not only to succeed but also to persevere in working with complex problems to develop their mathematical understanding. Proof outlines can provide students with guidance as they generate proofs, without reducing the complexity of an activity that can lead to deeper understanding.

Before students launch into the task of generating a proof, you can have a class discussion about the necessary steps for completing the proof. It is important to write the outline in such a way that students will still need to discuss their ideas and work together to fill in each step of the outline with mathematical statements, definitions, or theorems. A proof outline for the general formula for the sum of an infinite geometric series would look something like the following:

1. First, think about the sum of a finite geometric series such as $a + a \cdot r + a \cdot r^2 + a \cdot r^3 + \ldots + a \cdot r^{n-1} = S_n$, where S_n is some real number and $|r| < 1$. This step follows from the assumption that the finite geometric series has a sum because it is a convergent series.

2. To simplify this sum, note that all terms except the first term have a factor of r. Create a new equation that could be added to or subtracted from the equation in step 1 to simplify terms in the series. (Note: if students have derived the formula for the sum of n natural numbers by using the method of Gauss, suggest that they think about how a similar method could be applied here. The important thing is to let them discover a way to set up a system of equations to help them simplify, instead of telling them to multiply both sides of the first equation by r.)

3. Solve this simplified equation for S_n to get $S_n = \dfrac{a - ar^n}{1 - r}$.

4. Think about what happens to r^n as n goes to infinity. What does the value of r^n get close to? Use your thinking to reason why the expression $\dfrac{a}{1-r}$ can be used in finding the sum of the infinite geometric series.

Making proving routine

In our classroom vignette, the teacher provides an activity to help students reason about the sums of geometric series, and one student, Todd, blurts out a formula for use before the formula has been derived. Such an occurrence is common in classrooms—students may see a formula when following along in a textbook or may know a formula from another course or from working with a parent, tutor, friend, or sibling. The teacher in the vignette makes a crucial move to support the value of proof in the classroom culture. She acknowledges Todd's contribution—"You're right, Todd, that the formula you read can be used to find the sum of the first 200 terms of our series." At the same time, she emphasizes the importance of validating the formula before using it to solve problems—"we need to understand why the formula works before we can use it." She then engages the class in verifying the formula.

It may not always be the case that students understand the concepts and definitions that they would need to apply to successfully generate a proof for a theorem or formula that they will use. When developing a classroom culture where proof is valued and

Establishing a Classroom Culture Tip 1

Make proving a regular part of classroom work.

students are encouraged to reason about and explain ideas, students might still want to understand why something is true, even when they are not conceptually ready to generate a proof. In these situations, teachers can be explicit about the fact that students might not be able to generate a proof at that point in the course. In some cases, teachers might table a discussion of why a statement is true until later. Ultimately, whether students are ready to prove a statement or not, it is important for them to know that mathematics is powerful because the ideas and procedures on which it relies have been proven true or, in the case of axioms, have been accepted by mathematicians as true.

Modifying problems as proving opportunities

Because most high school curricula emphasize proof in a geometry course, curricular materials for other high school mathematics courses, such as algebra and precalculus, tend not to provide many tasks written explicitly to elicit justifications and proofs. The following are two general principles for modifying tasks to increase their proving potential:

1. Have students investigate mathematics through exploratory, pattern-generating activities that motivate them to make conjectures.

2. Reduce scaffolding that leads students step-by-step through a proof, instead making students responsible for reasoning through a proof.

The NCTM Illuminations website is an excellent online source for rich tasks with prompts that can be used or modified to increase their reasoning and proving potential. Books in NCTM's Focus in High School Mathematics series also provide examples of proof-rich tasks across a variety of content areas, including probability and statistics.

In our vignette of a class exploring the sum of a geometric series, the teacher first engages the students in exploring whether the sum would converge or diverge, as well as conjecturing about what the sum of the infinite series would be, by guiding them to create a table to keep track of partial sums of the infinite series. These moves correspond with the two principles of task modification above. These principles can be applied across a variety of mathematical topics.

For example, as an illustration of how to modify a task to motivate students to generate a proof, consider the following problem from a unit on quadratic functions:

Describe the behavior of the graph of $f(x) = ax^2 + bx + c$ as a, b, and c vary.

The task as stated does not require students to prove the patterns that they notice in the graph as a, b, and c vary but simply to describe the behavior. Students may check several sample cases where a, b, and c vary to get a sense of how the graph changes when each quantity changes, but the task does not direct them to attend to shifts in particular aspects of the graph, such as the position of the vertex, or to generate a conjecture about the general relationship between the coefficients of a quadratic function and its graph.

A few simple modifications can transform the task into a richer opportunity for proving. Consider the following problem:

> Given a parabola represented in standard form by $f(x) = ax^2 + bx + c$, investigate the effect of a, b, and c on the shape of the graph.
>
> Determine the equation that describes the locus of the vertex when $a = 1$ and $c = 1$, and justify that your equation is valid.

The potential of this task to engage students in proving increases as a result of three modifications in what students are asked to do. The modified problem calls for them to (1) make observations before they engage in proving activities; (2) make or revise conjectures, and (3) provide a mathematical argument or proof. When the students have completed the task and the whole class is reviewing students' work, not only will the students have investigated the behavior of varying values for a, b, and c, but they will also have produced a generalization (in equation form) of the locus of the vertex and potentially will have attempted an algebraic justification of the equation. The modified problem thus sets the stage for the emergence of situations for proving during class discussion.

Learning Goal 2: Understanding the Limitations of Examples

Big Idea 4 and Essential Understanding 4b emphasize that examples are a critical part of the proving process but do not suffice for establishing that something is true in mathematics. Chapter 2 illustrated the way in which students typically use examples when justifying their mathematical reasoning. In Ms. Tuttle's class, students rely on a table of values and quadratic regression to show that the ratio of the areas of the triangles is a quadratic relationship. Even students who are reasoning at a fairly sophisticated level may still resort to empirical evidence. To support our second learning goal—helping students recognize the limitations of examples—we offer some suggestions for aiding students in developing proofs that use logical and deductive forms of argumentation.

Big Idea 4

A proof is not an argument based on authority, perception, popular consensus, intuition, probability, or examples.

Essential
Understanding 4b
Examples can be a critical part of the proving process but do not suffice as a mathematical proof, except in the case of proof by exhaustion or proof by counterexample.

tip

**Designing
Problems and
Activities Tip 2**

*Introduce problems
for which
examples fail.*

Providing problems for which examples fail

The following tasks, adapted from Stylianides and Stylianides (2009), are examples of problems that are mathematically accessible for students with a range of mathematical abilities but also open the door for discussions of the limitations of examples-based reasoning.

Figure 3.1 presents the Circle and Spots problem (Stylianides and Stylianides 2009, p. 329), which challenges students' beliefs about empirical arguments. The pattern that emerges when students place and connect 2, 3, 4, and 5 dots around a circle does not hold for the case of 6 dots. In the cases of dots 2 through 5, the pattern appears to be $\frac{n(n+1)}{2}$ lines for n dots. However, for 6 dots, the number of non-overlapping regions is 31.

> Place different numbers of spots around a circle and join each pair of spots by straight lines. Explore a possible relation between the number of spots and the greatest number of nonoverlapping regions into which the circle can be divided by this means.
>
> *When there are 15 spots around the circle, is there an easy way to tell for sure what is the greatest number of nonoverlapping regions into which the circle can be divided?*

Fig. 3.1. The Circle and Spots problem (Stylianides and Stylianides 2009, p. 329)

A secondary but important opportunity afforded by the Circle and Spots problem comes from its use of imprecise language: "spots," "placed around the circle," and "non-overlapping." When attempting this task, students are very likely to ask for clarification about what "spots" are; whether placing the spots "around the circle" means inside the circle, on the circumference, or outside the area bounded by the circle; and how to identify "non-overlapping regions." The vagueness of these terms in the task prompt is purposeful; it opens up an opportunity to teach the importance of agreeing on the meaning of terms in a statement and using precise mathematical language. Below is a sample of how such a discussion might unfold:

Jane: I'm confused—what are "spots"? Are those like points?

Mr. Brown: Great question. Before you start to reason about a problem, it is always important that you are one-hundred-percent clear on the meaning of the terms. In math, what do we call things that look like spots?

Brittney: I think they just mean "points."

Mr. Brown: OK, so I'm going to change this statement to say "points" instead of "spots." Does anyone not want me to make this change? [*No one challenges the change.*]

Greg: So, is putting the spots "around the circle" like drawing points on the outside or on the circumference of the circle?

Mr. Brown: Well, let's see if it matters—draw two separate circles that don't overlap on your paper. On one circle, let's draw three points around the outside of one circle, and then let's use the other circle to investigate Greg's question by drawing those same points in similar positions on the circumference [*demonstrates on the board*]. If we connect the points with line segments, is the number of regions the same in each case?

Shelley: Well, not really, if you consider the parts that are created outside the circle.

Mr. Brown: OK, so what is it that we are trying to figure out in this problem?

Jane: The greatest number of non-overlapping regions the circle can be divided into with 15 points.

Mr. Brown: So, since we are interested in the number of regions the circle can be divided into, we should place our points on the circumference so that we don't get any extra regions outside of the circle.

The Circle and Spots problem provides students with an experience in which a perceived pattern fails after a few examples. Students may begin questioning the worth of determining a statement's truth-value by checking to see whether it works for a few cases. However, they still may believe that if you test a large number of cases and the statement holds, it is true. Reflect 3.2 presents a problem that Stylianides and Stylianides (2009) call "The Monstrous Counterexample," designed to reduce students' tendencies to believe that a critical mass of examples shows that a statement is true.

Reflect 3.2

Consider the following statement:

The expression $1 + 1141n^2$ (where n is a natural number) *never* gives a square number. (Stylianides and Stylianides 2009, p. 330)

Will this expression always give a non-square number, for any natural number n?

Most students will compute the expression with several natural numbers to see if they get a square number. Some students may try special cases, such as starting with the smallest natural number, 1, then trying a large number (say, 10,001), and then maybe trying a range of square numbers (say, 4, 64, 144). After a few minutes of exploration, students can discuss whether they think the statement is true.

On the basis of their investigations, students are likely to say that the statement is either true or probably true (if they have begun to question the validity of examples-based reasoning). Then the teacher can reveal the following information:

> People used computers to check this expression and found out that it does not give a square number for any natural number from 1 to 30,693,385,322,765,657,197,397,207.
>   BUT
> It gives a square number for the next natural number! (From Stylianides and Stylianides [2009, p. 330])

Not only does the Monstrous Counterexample problem provide a case for which empirical reasoning is likely to be inadequate, since it is not humanly feasible to check enough examples, but it also provides an opportunity to discuss the role of counterexamples in mathematical proof. Although generating a few confirming examples cannot show that a statement is true for all cases, a single contrary example can show that a statement is false.

For mathematicians, finding a counterexample to show that a statement is false can open the door to refining the conjecture so that it is a true statement. If we think of the proving process as consisting of finding a pattern, generating a conjecture, and producing a proof (G. Stylianides 2009), then discovering a counterexample can turn the cycle back to generating a new conjecture to be proven true. However, in each and every cycle of the proving process, a logical argument based on definitions, axioms, proven statements, and theorems is the basis for showing that something is true, whereas examples—even just a single example—can show a statement to be false.

One way to build on students' new understandings about mathematical proof as a result of exploring the Circle and Spots and the Monstrous Counterexample problems is to have students work on a task that elicits their empirical reasoning but is at a conceptual level at which a mathematical proof is within their reach. One example of such a task is the Squares problem (Stylianides and Stylianides 2009, p. 328), which is the focus of Reflect 3.3.

Reflect 3.3

In the Squares problem shown below from Stylianides and Stylianides (2009, p. 328), how many 2-by-2 squares are in the 4-by-4 square? How many 3-by-3 squares are in the 4-by-4 square?

1. Find the number of all different squares.

2. What if this was a 5-by-5 square?

3. What if this was a 60-by-60 square? How would you work to find how many different squares there would be? How would you make sure that you found them all?

How does modifying the Squares problem in this way help students to understand how squares of different side lengths exist within the larger 4-by-4 square?

In the Squares problem, students begin in part 1 to explore the number of different squares for a particular case, a 4-by-4 square. Part 2 involves students in considering a 5-by-5 square, and part 3 engages them in investigating a much larger case—a 60-by-60 square. The advantage of asking students about the 60-by-60 square is that they cannot resort to drawing the case and counting the squares empirically. You might imagine a student providing the following justification when asked about the 60-by-60 case:

So, for a 4-by-4 there are 16 total squares, and for a 5-by-5 there are 25 squares. You just keep adding an extra square to each row and column, so the pattern isn't going to change. So, for a 60-by-60 square, there are 60^2, or 3600, squares of sizes 2 by 2, 3 by 3, and so on.

Although students are unlikely to attempt to draw a 60-by-60 square to find the answer in part 3, research shows that most students are likely to decide that the pattern $\sum_{n=1}^{k} n^2$ holds for the case of $n = 60$ because it was true for the 4-by-4 square and the 5-by-5 square. Thus, students begin the sequence of tasks by drawing on their intuitive beliefs about empirical arguments. The work of Stylianides and Stylianides (2009) suggests that most students are likely to point to the fact that the pattern worked for the 4-by-4 case and the 5-by-5 case to answer the question, "How would you make sure that you had found them all?" But some students are likely to indicate that they cannot be sure just by showing that the pattern is true for a set of cases.

Such a moment is opportune for a teacher to remind students of what they found in the Circle and Spots problem and the Monstrous Counterexample. Students will then be likely to recognize that they are relying on a few cases to believe that something is true. Although recognizing the limits of empirical reasoning is crucial, it does not guarantee that students will be able to produce a deductive argument.

Asking for *explanations why* instead of *demonstrations that*

Teaching Moves Tip 2

Ask students to explain why rather than show that it works.

In working with the Squares problem, students will initially demonstrate how they count all of the possible squares when answering the question, "How do you know that you have found them all?" Shifting the question to, "Why are you sure that you have them all?" focuses students' attention on considering the reasoning that underlies the pattern that they see in their examples. When confronted with this question, students are likely to become frustrated or to struggle to articulate their reasoning. Once again, a proof outline can be a great tool, providing some scaffolding to help students generate a deductive argument. The following proof outline could be used to structure a class discussion on the Squares problem:

1. In a 60-by-60 square, we have squares of sizes k-by-k, where $1 \leq k \leq 60$ and k is a natural number.

2. To find the total number of different squares in a 60-by-60 square, we need to add the numbers of squares of all different sizes.

3. The formula $(60 - k + 1)^2$ gives the number of squares of each size.

4. We add the numbers given by the formula for every value of k to get the total number of different squares in a 60-by-60 square. This gives us $1^2 + 2^2 + 3^2 + \ldots + 58^2 + 59^2 + 60^2$. (Adapted from Stylianides and Stylianides 2009, p. 346)

In step 3 of the proof outline, students need to elaborate on how to obtain the formula for the number of squares of each size. Alternatively, teachers could present step 3 simply as, "Find the formula for the number of squares of each size," and students could complete the proof initially as a small-group activity, followed by a whole-group discussion of explanations for step 3.

Research tells us that reliance on empirical arguments is often persistent, even after students complete a high school geometry course or while they are taking a undergraduate course focused on learning to prove. However, the sequence of tasks in the Squares problem has been shown to be effective in challenging these beliefs in high school students (A. Stylianides 2009) as well as in preservice elementary teachers (Stylianides and Stylianides 2009). An important point to underscore is that students should not be told to avoid generating examples when they are producing conjectures or even when they are attempting to justify conjectures. As we will discuss further, examples can play a powerful role in helping students understand and articulate their mathematical thinking.

Learning Goal 3: Moving beyond Examples-Based Arguments to Deductive Proofs

Although relying on confirming examples when producing a proof is mathematically invalid, engaging in empirical investigations and testing cases is a *necessary* part of learning mathematics with understanding. Examples can contribute productively to students' proving in two ways. First, generating examples can involve translating an abstract mathematical statement into a concrete case. The act of producing a correct example of a statement indicates a basic level of understanding of the meaning of the statement, and producing several examples can help students discover the relationships between the mathematical objects in the statement. For example, when students produce the examples $2 + 3 = 5$, $14 + 15 = 29$, and $16 + 17 = 23$ when thinking about how to prove the statement, "The sum of two consecutive numbers is an odd number," they illustrate an understanding of what consecutive numbers are. Producing a sequence of such examples may help students recognize that two consecutive numbers differ by 1, so the sum can be represented as $n + n + 1$, or $2n + 1$, for any integer value n.

Building from examples to conjectures

A second way in which examples can contribute productively to students' proving is by facilitating the conjecturing process. One typical way in which students encounter examples that lead to conjectures, especially in beginning algebra courses, is by investigating number in relation to visual patterns, as in the Hexagon Patterns task (see fig. 3.2).

> **Designing Problems and Activities Tip 3**
>
> *Create tasks where examples can help generate conjectures.*

Given such patterning tasks, students often have difficulties in generating a conjecture that relates the rate of change in the pattern to the stage number. As a result, students tend, at least initially, to produce a generalization that is a recursive rule—for instance, in this case, the perimeter of a row of hexagon tables is found by adding 5

1. Suppose you arrange hexagonal tables in a row, where the tables all have side length of 1 unit. Compute the perimeter for tables in stages 1–4.

2. What would be the perimeter of the row of 50 hexagonal tables? Explain how you know that your answer is correct.

Fig. 3.2. Hexagon Patterns task

to the perimeter of the previous row of hexagon tables. However, a recursive rule cannot be proved with a deductive argument.

Work by Ellis (2007) suggests that having students reason about problems that require them to think about how real-world quantities (such as height, time, distance, length, or speed) are related to one another can help them create generalizations that they can prove deductively. Two easy modifications of the Hexagon Patterns task in figure 3.2 can help students reason with quantities. First, instead of providing them with pictures of the arrangement of one, two, three, and four tables, teachers can give students popsicle sticks to construct the figures on their own. By constructing each stage, they can more easily recognize the relationship between the number of sticks necessary to add another table and the change in the perimeter. Encouraging students to create a chart such as the one in figure 3.3 can also help them keep track of the related quantities.

Number of tables (n)	Perimeter	Unit increase in perimeter
1	6	
2	10	4
3	14	4

Fig. 3.3. A chart of values for the Hexagon Patterns task

The chart in the figure is an example of modeling a problem's *situation*, as opposed to modeling a problem's *solution* (Smith 2004). To reason deductively, students using the chart need to justify why the perimeter increases by 4 each time. An example of a possible justification follows:

Since the tables are regular hexagons, only one side of the table already there meets up with one side of the new table added. As a result, these sides are not a part of the total perimeter count. So, even though a table of 6 sides is being added, 2 sides are not a part of the perimeter, so the overall change in the perimeter is 4 units.

Once students establish why the pattern can be assumed to hold no matter how many tables are added, they may then be able justify a rule to find the perimeter of n tables, as follows:

Each time I add a new table, it adds 4 more units to the perimeter. So, if I do this n times, I am actually adding on $4(n - 1)$, since I don't add anything to the first table. The first table's perimeter was 6, so the equation for the perimeter of n tables is $6 + 4(n - 1)$. This simplifies to $4n + 2$.

Making a conjecture wall

Another important use of examples in the classroom is to motivate students to explore and generate conjectures (Watson and Mason 2005) and thus "foster mathematical curiosity" (Knuth 2002). Students' empirical investigations often lead them to discover patterns that, although not the intended outcome of an activity, are still intellectually interesting and often true. "Conjecture walls," on which students can post conjectures that they discover but may not be able to prove at the time, can be useful classroom resources for encouraging mathematical inquisitiveness. For example, after students learn about the rules of exponents, the teacher might use the following problem at the beginning of a lesson or as a warm-up problem:

Consider statements 1, 2, and 3 below. Are they true? Why?

1. $2^1, 2^2, 2^3, \ldots 2^{99}$ cannot be multiples of 10.

2. $1^{99} + 2^{99} + 3^{99}$ cannot be an even number.

3. $1^x + 2^x + 3^x + 4^x + 5^x$ is a multiple of 5 when x is odd.

Having students evaluate each of these statements can be a way to reinforce students' understanding of exponents or assess their understanding (as described later, in the section Assessing Students' Understanding of Proof). Not only will students use examples to help them understand the mathematical claim in each statement—testing for $x = 3$, for instance, in the case of statement 3. But also each statement is structured in such a way to suggest other types of patterns that students can generate on their own, related to raising numbers to exponential powers.

For example, students may consider whether $1^x + 2^x + 3^x + 4^x$ is a multiple of 4 when x is odd or whether $2^{99} + 3^{99}$ is an odd

Building a Classroom Culture Tip 2

Create a conjecture wall.

number. Being able to construct their own mathematical statements helps students experience mathematics as more meaningful and personal.

Using examples is an important part of the process of doing mathematics, but students also have to learn that showing that a statement holds for a few examples shows only that it is at least sometimes true instead of proving that it is always true. Using problems like Circle and Spots and the Monstrous Counterexample can help students understand the limitations of examples, but we also need to do more to help students learn how to write deductive and logically rigorous proofs.

Clarifying the criteria for a valid proof

Teaching Moves Tip 3

Make explicit what is needed for a proof to be valid.

Embedded in Big Idea 2 is the notion that mathematical proof is different from other types of proof, such as those that have validity in legal settings or in the physical sciences. Our discussion of Big Idea 2 touched on these differences. Part of the mathematics teacher's role is to make explicit to students what counts as proof in the discipline of mathematics. Teachers can perform this role effectively by having a classroom discussion about criteria that will be used to standardize the kinds of proofs that students generate in class.

Big Idea 2

A proof is a specific type of mathematical argument, which is a connected sequence of deductive, logical statements in support of or against a mathematical claim.

Establishing criteria for valid mathematical proof is an important activity and should take place early in the school year. One way to start this classroom conversation is to ask for a proof of a mathematical statement that can be understood easily by most members of the class. An ideal statement is one that lends itself to a variety of different types of proofs. One such statement is,

$$1 + 3 + 5 + \ldots + (2n - 1) = n^2,$$

where n is a non-negative integer. Some students will generate justifications that feature only examples, while other students may try to use what they know about odd numbers and the sum of the first n natural numbers,

$$\frac{n(n + 1)}{2},$$

to produce a justification.

Building a Classroom Culture Tip 3

Create and display "Criteria for Mathematical Proof."

Students can then write different justifications on the board, comparing and contrasting them while noting how features of the justifications do or do not show that the statement is true for all possible values of n. The goal of this discussion should be to develop some general criteria for judging the validity of a proof, no matter what statement is being proved. Below is an example of such criteria (Stylianides and Al-Murani 2010, p. 24); however, keep in mind that each class may develop different criteria, and the criteria can be modified as students become more familiar with processes for writing and evaluating proofs.

Criteria for Mathematical Proof

1. It can be used to convince not only myself or a friend but also a [skeptic]. It should not require someone to make a leap of faith (e.g., "This is how it is" or "You need to believe me that this [pattern] will go on forever.")

2. It should help someone understand why a statement is true (e.g., why a pattern works the way it does).

3. It should use ideas that our class knows already or is able to understand (e.g., equations, pictures, diagrams).

4. It should contain no errors (e.g., in calculations).

5. It should be clearly presented.

Once some initial criteria for mathematical proof have been established, students can begin to use them when evaluating their own and one another's proofs.

Asking for a different approach

If students are still in the process of learning key concepts and definitions for a statement that they are being asked to prove, such as a statement about sums of odd numbers or angles formed when parallel lines are cut by a transversal, a natural tendency is to generate supporting examples. One activity that can help students think differently about justifying a statement is to ask them to do it another way. Either provide an examples-based proof or discuss an examples-based proof generated by a student, and then give the class the task of writing a different argument. For this technique to be successful, it is important to be specific about what has to be different about the students' new justifications. Explaining what new information they need to include, such as the use of the definition of certain terms in the statement, is as important as telling them what their justification should exclude, such as examples.

Designing Problems and Activities Tip 4

"Do it a different way."

Having students make sense of peers' proofs

It is vitally important that students have regular opportunities to make sense of one another's proofs—not only for developing their skills in generating and evaluating proofs, but also for helping them understand the necessity of doing proof in classrooms. As a class, students should reach a consensus on the validity of a statement on the basis of a shared understanding of why it is valid.

One drawback to having students discuss one another's arguments on a regular basis is that facilitating such a discussion requires quite a bit of class time. A timesaving strategy is to collect students' justifications on exit slips at the end of class and select a

Teaching Moves Tip 4

Have students make sense of one another's proofs.

range of justifications to present at the beginning of the next day's lesson. Carefully selected responses can be efficiently presented by means of an overhead projector, an interactive whiteboard, or a document camera, and they will remind students of their work the day before. Students should take a few minutes to evaluate each justification according to the class's criteria for mathematical proof. Then selected students can share what they noticed about a particular justification and whether or not they believe that it is a valid proof. Opening the class with this discussion can have a positive effect on the justifications that students produce throughout the day's lesson.

To get a sense of how this process might work in a classroom, consider the End Cap Math task, shown in figure 3.4 (adapted from a Calendar Problem in *Mathematics Teacher*). Figure 3.5 shows some sample student responses to the task (obtained from the *Mathematics Teacher* problem database at http://www.nctm.org /publications/calendar/default.aspx?journal_id=2).

End Cap Math

A grocer makes a display of cans in which the top row has one can and each subsequent row has two more cans than the row above it.

Write a rule to determine the number of rows a display will contain if it is made up of *n* cans. What kind of number must *n* be to create such a display?

Fig. 3.4. End Cap Math task, adapted from a *Mathematics Teacher* Calendar Problem (August 2005)

Building a Classroom Culture Tip 4

Use a rubric to help students evaluate proofs.

Rubrics can help students learn how to use the class's criteria for mathematical proof to evaluate one another's arguments. A rubric like the one shown in figure 3.6 might be given to students to review before they evaluate the three student responses for the End Cap Math task in figure 3.5.

After students have reviewed the rubric and the responses, they can discuss how they would rate the responses (non-proof, rationale, and proof). During the discussion, students can be encouraged to explain why they would place a response in a particular category. Once the students have reached a consensus about how to categorize a particular response, the teacher can press them to suggest ways to improve the response so that it could be categorized as a proof.

For example, students might argue that response 1 is a non-proof because the answer is wrong. Guiding them to use the rubric might help them focus on the representation or type of argument, catalyzing a more productive discussion than if they simply dismiss an argument because the answer happens to be incorrect.

Student Response 1

The display will always have 1 can at the top. The next row will have 3 cans, and the row after that will have 5 cans. You will get consecutive odd numbers for each row because if you add 2 to an odd number, you get the next odd number. Since there are $\frac{n}{2}$ odd numbers in n, the number of rows is $\frac{n}{2}$.

Student Response 2

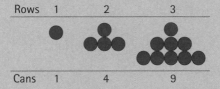

So, n cans will make up $\sqrt{n}$ rows. Then, n has to be a perfect square.

Student Response 3

I drew the picture below to show how the cans are arranged:

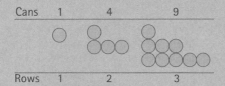

For each row added, the total number of cans equals the row number squared. To show this, I rearranged the cans in the picture below:

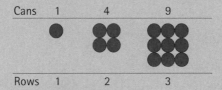

If there are n cans, there must be $\sqrt{n}$ rows. So, n must be a perfect square to make the display with no extra cans.

Fig. 3.5. Three sample student solutions for the
End Cap Math problem

	Non-proof	Rationale	Proof
Type of argument	• Shows only examples • Restates given statement	• Explains how but not why • Draws a picture without providing an explanation of why the statement is true • May use logical reasoning but is not deductive	• Explains why statement is true for all cases • Uses logical, deductive reasoning (doesn't require a leap of faith) • Does not use examples
Representation of argument	• Does not use pictures, diagrams, words, or equations that can be understood by the class	• Uses pictures, diagrams, words, or equations that can be understood by the class	• Uses pictures, diagrams, words, or equations that can be understood by the class
Mathematical validity of argument	• Contains one or more mathematical errors	• Does not contain math errors but is not a complete explanation	• Does not contain mathematical errors • Covers all possible cases

Fig. 3.6. Rubric emphasizing the criteria for proof

In fact, response 1 presents an argument that is *not* examples-based or a simple restatement of something that is given. To its credit, the argument uses general statements that apply beyond a specific case. Also, the narrative form of the argument is a valid approach. The argument is a non-proof because it lacks mathematical validity. The focus of the discussion could then turn to the logical error in the argument in relating the number of odd numbers less than n with the total number of rows needed to make the display.

Assessing Students' Understanding of Proof

An obvious way to assess students' understanding of proving and their ability to prove is to ask them to generate a proof, either as a class activity or on a quiz or test. Students' ability to produce a proof involves orchestrating their understanding of the task (including the given information, which they can assume to be true), generating and logically sequencing statements that are given or known to be true, and evaluating whether the argument is complete. Students' success depends on their understanding of the mathematical content of the statement and their ability to carry out the various aspects of this complex activity. Mathematicians who have produced many valid proofs over their careers continually encounter situations in which generating a proof is a difficult, if not impossible, task. The learning goals outlined in this chapter suggest ways of formatively assessing students' progress in developing the knowledge, skills, and beliefs to succeed in generating a proof. Assessment items can incorporate tasks that go beyond simply asking students to produce a proof to providing them with opportunities that teachers can use to determine their progress toward particular learning goals for proof.

Incorporating proving in quizzes and exams

One of the key learning goals presented in this chapter is to understand the limitations of examples-based reasoning. It is not necessary to ask students to produce a justification or proof to assess whether or not they understand that mathematical proof should not be based on empirical evidence. Creating a proof is a complex task, and students can recognize when an argument is not sufficient as proof, even though they may not be able to generate a valid proof. An alternative way to assess students' progress in understanding the limitations of examples-based reasoning is to ask them to evaluate a set of given justifications for a mathematical statement. Figure 3.7 provides an example of such a task that could be incorporated into an exam in an algebra course.

Figure 3.7 shows two arguments in response to the proof evaluation task presented in the figure. Anne's argument is an example of an algebraic proof; Marcus's argument is examples-based. An important feature of the task is that it prompts students not only to discuss whether the given arguments are valid proofs, but also to provide reasons why. Furthermore, the wording of the prompt—"write a paragraph discussing whether [Anne's and Marcus's] responses are valid proofs"—leaves open the possibility that both arguments are valid. This increases the likelihood that students will not choose an argument just because it has more words or symbols.

Assessment Tip 1

Incorporate tasks into regular exams that assess students' progress in learning goals for reasoning and proving.

Two students, Anne and Marcus, have been asked to justify why the method of completing the square is a valid method to factor a quadratic expression. They have been specifically asked to prove why $x^2 + ax = \left(x + \dfrac{a}{2}\right)^2 - \left(\dfrac{a}{2}\right)^2$, for any real values of x and a. Their responses are shown below. Write a paragraph discussing whether their responses are valid proofs. Provide evidence from each student's response to justify your argument.

Anne's Response

To complete the square, you would need to add a term to $x^2 + ax$ so that it would become a perfect square trinomial of the form $a^2 + 2ab + b^2$. If $x^2 = a^2$, then $ax = 2ab$. So $b = \left(\dfrac{x}{2}\right)$. Since I assumed $x^2 = a^2$, then I can claim $x = a$. So $b = \left(\dfrac{a}{2}\right)$. To transform $x^2 + ax$ into a perfect square trinomial, I would need to add $b^2 = \left(\dfrac{a}{2}\right)^2$. The perfect square trinomial now becomes $x^2 + ax + \left(\dfrac{a}{2}\right)^2$. Since I added in the quantity $\left(\dfrac{a}{2}\right)^2$, I have to make sure to subtract it, so the value of the expression does not change: $\left(x + \dfrac{a}{2}\right)^2 - \left(\dfrac{a}{2}\right)^2$.

Marcus's Response

If $a = 1$, then $x^2 + ax = x^2 + x$. And $\left(x + \dfrac{a}{2}\right)^2 - \left(\dfrac{a}{2}\right)^2 = \left(x + \dfrac{1}{2}\right)^2 - \left(\dfrac{1}{2}\right)^2$. I simplified the right-hand side to get $x^2 + x + \dfrac{1}{4} - \dfrac{1}{4}$, which equals $x^2 + x$. Since both sides are the same, they must be equal. It works if $a = -1$, too: $\left(x - \dfrac{1}{2}\right)^2 - \left(\dfrac{-1}{2}\right)^2 = \left(x - \dfrac{1}{2}\right)^2 - \dfrac{1}{4}$. This simplifies to $x^2 - x + \dfrac{1}{4} - \dfrac{1}{4}$, which equals $x^2 - x$. Since it works for positive and negative values of a, it always works.

Fig. 3.7. A proof evaluation task and two responses

The most important aspect of this task is that, as discussed in relation to Essential Understanding 1*a*, the content of the task is a fundamental part of the algebra curriculum—namely, learning to complete the square. It is not a special theorem or a unique problem; rather, the prompt to evaluate the arguments encourages students to think conceptually about the algebraic operations involved in completing the square. Incorporating reasoning and proving tasks into the curriculum, whether during a lesson or during a unit exam, engages students in developing conceptual understanding.

Distinguishing levels of proficiency in students' proving

Writing a valid deductive proof requires that students have sufficient content knowledge to understand meanings of definitions, recall and employ appropriate axioms, prove statements and theorems, and present an argument in a clear and logical sequence. Doing this successfully is a difficult task, especially under the pressure of a timed exam! Incorporating sub-items into a proof task on quizzes or unit tests that assess students' understanding of important definitions and axioms can provide teachers with valuable information to guide future instruction, as well as potentially aiding students in recognizing the importance of referring to definitions when generating a proof in response to a task. Figure 3.8 shows such an assessment task for a unit on vertical, complementary, and supplementary angles.

A student with a beginning understanding of the definition of supplementary angles and properties of intersecting lines might respond to part (a) by writing the following: "$\angle DBA$ and $\angle CBD$ sum to make a straight line because line DE intersects line AC." In contrast, a student with a proficient understanding might respond in the following way:

> $\angle DBA$ and $\angle CBD$ are supplementary angles. They are formed by line DE intersecting line AC. Since AC is a line, the measure of $\angle CBA$ is 180°. Then $m\angle DBA$ and $m\angle CBD$ sum to 180° and are supplementary by the definition of supplementary angles.

The student with a beginning understanding of applying definitions and the student with a more proficient understanding differ in the extent to which they refer to definitions in constructing logical arguments. The beginning student's response makes observations about features of the given picture without relating them back to definitions or theorems regarding general geometric properties. Nor does the student provide a complete argument to justify the claim that "$\angle DBA$ and $\angle CBD$ sum to make a straight line." In contrast, the proficient student's response begins by immediately

Essential Understanding 1*a*
The processes of proving include a variety of activities, such as developing conjectures, considering the general case, exploring with examples, looking for structural similarities across cases, and searching for counterexamples.

Assessment Tip 2
Evaluate the extent to which students' arguments refer to relevant and proven statements, axioms, and definitions.

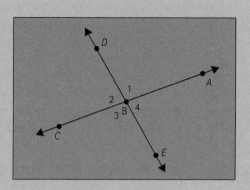

Summarize the Mathematics

In this investigation, you used deductive reasoning to establish relationships between pairs of angles formed by two intersecting lines. In the diagram, suppose the lines intersect so that $m\angle DBA = m\angle CBD$.

a. What can you conclude about these two angles? Prepare an argument to prove your conjecture.

b. What can you conclude about the other angles in the diagram? Write a proof of your conclusion.

c. What mathematical facts did you use to help prove your statements in Parts *a* and *b*? Were these facts definitions, postulates, or theorems?

d. Describe the relationship between $\overleftrightarrow{AC}$ and $\overleftrightarrow{DE}$.

Be prepared to share your conjectures and explain your proofs.

Fig. 3.8. The relationship between angles formed by perpendicular lines (Coxford et al. 2009, p. 34)

making the claim that the angles are supplementary and then provides evidence from the given information to support the claim in a logical manner.

Students rarely need to produce a proof when responding to an open-ended item on a state or national standardized assessment. To ensure that students are developing competencies to be successful in proving as they take higher-level mathematics courses, teachers must give classroom assessments that go beyond simply asking students to provide a proof. Planning specific tasks to assess a range of competencies related to proof—whether they are intended as "entry slips" or warm-ups at the beginning of class or as questions on an end-of-chapter test—ensures that students will have opportunities to use their knowledge in a variety of different contexts. Developing rubrics such as the one shown in figure 3.6 can be a way both to help students learn the norms of valid mathematical proof and to determine whether a student is at a beginning, proficient, or advanced level in generating and evaluating mathematical arguments. Including proof-related questions on each assessment is essential if students are to understand that proving is an important part of doing mathematics.

Conclusion

This chapter has presented a variety of suggestions for using particular teaching moves, designing problems and activities, and building a classroom culture to support three overarching goals for students' learning about proof: (1) developing fluency in proving, (2) understanding the limitations of examples, and (3) moving beyond examples-based arguments to construct deductive proofs. Several vignettes have demonstrated how the suggested teaching moves and tasks could support students in achieving the three key goals, and strategies for assessing students' progress have been explored.

Throughout this book, we have discussed the underlying knowledge and beliefs needed to understand mathematical proof, as well as different strategies for helping students engage in the complex activity of mathematical proof. We have highlighted the notion that doing mathematical proof is not only about the final product—a written set of statements or a picture demonstrating the validity of a conjecture—but also about developing the mathematical habits of mind to approach mathematical situations by recognizing patterns, developing generalizations and conjectures, and generating mathematical arguments that convince others—as well as oneself—that a conjecture is true.

References

Balacheff, Nicolas. "Processus de Preuve et Situations de Validation" [Proving processes and situations for validation]. *Educational Studies in Mathematics* 18 (May 1987): 147–76.

Barnett-Clarke, Carne, William Fisher, Rick Marks, and Sharon Ross. *Developing Essential Understanding of Rational Numbers for Teaching Mathematics in Grades 3–5*. Essential Understanding Series. Reston, Va.: National Council of Teachers of Mathematics, 2010.

Bell, Alan W. "A Study of Pupil's Proof-Explanations in Mathematical Situations." *Educational Studies in Mathematics* 7 (July 1976): 23–40.

Cooney, Thomas P., Sybilla Beckmann, and Gwendolyn M. Lloyd. *Developing Essential Understanding of Functions for Teaching Mathematics in Grades 9–12*. Essential Understanding Series. Reston, Va.: National Council of Teachers of Mathematics, 2010.

Coxford, Arthur F., James T. Fey, Christian R. Hirsch, Harold L. Schoen, Gail Burrill, Eric W. Hart, and Ann E. Watkins. *Core-Plus Mathematics: Contemporary Mathematics in Context, Course 3*. 2nd ed. Columbus, Ohio: Glencoe/McGraw-Hill, 2009.

Dreyfus, Tommy. "Advanced Mathematical Thinking." In *Mathematics and Cognition: A Research Synthesis by the International Group for the Psychology of Mathematics Education*, edited by Pearla Nesher and Jeremy Kilpatrick, pp. 113–34. Cambridge: Cambridge University Press, 1990.

Ellis, Amy B. "Connections between Generalizing and Justifying: Students' Reasoning about Linear Relationships." *Journal for Research in Mathematics Education* 38 (May 2007): 194–229.

——. "The Proof Is in the Practice." *Mathematics Teaching in the Middle School* 16 (May 2011): 522–27.

Felton, Mathew D. "Context and Preservice Teachers' Conceptions of Proof: Accounting for Context in a Math Methods Lesson." Master's thesis, University of Wisconsin, 2007.

Hanna, Gila. *Rigorous Proof in Mathematics Education*. Toronto: OISE Press, 1983.

Hanna, Gila, Hans Niels Jahnke, and Helmut Pulte, eds. *Explanation and Proof in Mathematics: Philosophical and Educational Perspectives*. New York: Springer, 2009.

Harel, Guershon, and Larry Sowder. "Students' Proof Schemes." *Research on Collegiate Mathematics Education*, vol. 3, edited by Ed Dubinsky, Alan Schoenfeld, and James Kaput, pp. 234–83. Providence, R.I.: American Mathematical Society, 1998.

Herbst, Patricio, Gloriana Gonzalez, and Michele Macke. "How
    Can Geometry Students Learn What It Means to Define in
    Mathematics?" *The Mathematics Educator* 15 (Fall 2005):
    17–24.
Jurgensen, Ray C., Richard G. Brown, and John W. Jurgensen.
    Geometry. Boston: Houghton Mifflin, 1988.
Knuth, Eric. "Fostering Mathematical Curiosity." *Mathematics
    Teacher* 95 (February 2002): 126–30.
Knuth, Eric, Jeffrey Choppin, and Kristen Bieda. "Proof: Examples
    and Beyond." *Mathematics Teaching in the Middle School* 15
    (November 2009): 206–11.
Lakatos, Imre. "What Does a Mathematical Proof Prove?" In *New
    Directions in the Philosophy of Mathematics: An Anthology*,
    edited by Thomas Tymoczko, pp. 153–162. Princeton, N.J.:
    Princeton University Press, 1998.
Lannin, John, Amy B. Ellis, and Rebekah Elliott. *Developing
    Essential Understanding of Mathematical Reasoning for
    Teaching Mathematics in Prekindergarten–Grade 8*. Essential
    Understanding Series. Reston, Va.: National Council of Teachers
    of Mathematics, 2011.
Larson, Ron, Robert P. Hostetler, and Bruce Edwards. *Calculus of a
    Single Variable*. 7th ed. Boston: Houghton-Mifflin, 2002
Lawrence, Ann, and Charlie Hennessy. *Lessons for Algebraic
    Thinking: Grades 6–8*. Sausalito, Calif.: Math Solutions, 2002.
Lloyd, Gwendolyn M., Beth Herbel-Eisenmann, and Jon R. Star.
    *Developing Essential Understanding of Expressions, Equations,
    and Functions for Teaching Mathematics in Grades 6–8*.
    Essential Understanding Series. Reston, Va.: National Council of
    Teachers of Mathematics, 2011.
Lobato, Joanne, and Amy B. Ellis. *Developing Essential
    Understanding of Ratios, Proportions, and Proportional
    Reasoning for Teaching Mathematics in Grades 6–8*. Essential
    Understanding Series. Reston, Va.: National Council of
    Teachers of Mathematics, 2010.
National Council of Teachers of Mathematics (NCTM). *Principles
    and Standards for School Mathematics*. Reston, Va.: NCTM,
    2000.
——. *Curriculum Focal Points for Prekindergarten through Grade 8
    Mathematics: A Quest for Coherence*. Reston, Va.: NCTM, 2006.
——. *Focus in High School Mathematics: Reasoning and Sense
    Making*. Reston, Va.: NCTM, 2009.
Osler, Thomas J. "Proof without Words: Integral of Sine Squared."
    The AMATYC Review 24 (Fall 2002): 65.
Peck, Roxy, Robert Gould, and Steven Miller. *Developing Essential
    Understanding of Statistics for Teaching Mathematics in*

Grades 9–12. Essential Understanding Series. Reston, Va.: National Council of Teachers of Mathematics, forthcoming.

Schoenfeld, Alan. "What Do We Know about Mathematics Curricula?" *Journal of Mathematical Behavior* 13 (March 1994): 55–80.

Sekiguchi, Yasuhiro. "Mathematical Proof, Argumentation, and Classroom Communication: From a Cultural Perspective." *Tsukuba Journal of Educational Study in Mathematics* 21 (2002), 11–20.

Shaughnessy, J. Michael, Beth Chance, and Henry Kranendonk. *Focus in High School Mathematics: Reasoning and Sense Making in Statistics and Probability*. Focus in High School Mathematics series. Reston, Va.: National Council of Teachers of Mathematics, 2009.

Sinclair, Nathalie, David Pimm, and Melanie Skelin. *Developing Essential Understanding of Geometry for Teaching Mathematics in Grades 6–8*. Essential Understanding Series. Reston, Va.: National Council of Teachers of Mathematics, 2012.

———. *Developing Essential Understanding of Geometry for Teaching Mathematics in Grades 9–12*. Essential Understanding Series. Reston, Va.: National Council of Teachers of Mathematics, 2012.

Smith, Margaret. "Beyond Presenting Good Problems: How a Japanese Teacher Implements a Mathematics Task." In *Perspectives on the Teaching of Mathematics*, Sixty-sixth Yearbook of the National Council of Teachers of Mathematics (NCTM), edited by Rheta Rubenstein and George Bright, pp. 96–106. Reston, Va.: NCTM, 2004.

Stylianides, Andreas J. "Proof and Proving in School Mathematics." *Journal for Research in Mathematics Education* 38 (May 2007), 289–321.

———. "Breaking the Equation 'Empirical Argument = Proof.'" *Mathematics Teaching* 213 (March 2009): 9–14.

Stylianides, Andreas J., and Thabit Al-Murani. "Can a Proof and a Counterexample Coexist? Students' Conceptions about the Relationship between Proof and Refutation." *Research in Mathematics Education* 12 (March 2010): 21–36.

Stylianides, Gabriel J. "Reasoning-and-Proving in School Mathematics Textbooks." *Mathematical Thinking and Learning* 11, no. 4 (2009): 258–88.

Stylianides, Gabriel J., and Andreas J. Stylianides. "Facilitating the Transition from Empirical Arguments to Proof." *Journal for Research in Mathematics Education* 40 (May 2009): 314–52.

Sultan, Alan, and Alice F. Artzt. *The Mathematics That Every Secondary School Math Teacher Needs to Know*. New York: Routledge, 2010.

Tokyo Shoseki. 新編新しい数学2 [New mathematics 2]. Tokyo:
     Tokyo Shoseki, 1997.
Watson, Anne, and John Mason. *Mathematics as a Constructive
     Activity: Learners Generating Examples*. Mahwah, N.J.:
     Lawrence Erlbaum, 2005.
Weber, Keith. "Problem-Solving, Proving, and Learning: The
     Relationship between Problem-Solving Processes and Learning
     Opportunities in the Activity of Proof Construction." *Journal of
     Mathematical Behavior* 24, nos. 3–4 (2005): 351–60.

Titles in the Essential Understanding Series

The Essential Understanding Series gives teachers the deep understanding that they need to teach challenging topics in mathematics. Students encounter such topics across the pre-K–grade 12 curriculum, and teachers who understand the related big ideas can give maximum support as students develop their own understanding and make vital connections.

Developing Essential Understanding of—

Number and Numeration for Teaching Mathematics in Prekindergarten–Grade 2
 ISBN 978-0-87353-629-5   Stock No. 13492

Addition and Subtraction for Teaching Mathematics in Prekindergarten–Grade 2
 ISBN 978-0-87353-664-6   Stock No. 13792

Rational Numbers for Teaching Mathematics in Grades 3–5
 ISBN 978-0-87353-630-1   Stock No. 13493

Algebraic Thinking for Teaching Mathematics in Grades 3–5
 ISBN 978-0-87353-668-4   Stock No. 13796

Multiplication and Division for Teaching Mathematics in Grades 3–5
 ISBN 978-0-87353-667-7   Stock No. 13795

Ratios, Proportions, and Proportional Reasoning for Teaching Mathematics in Grades 6–8
 ISBN 978-0-87353-622-6   Stock No. 13482

Expressions, Equations, and Functions for Teaching Mathematics in Grades 6–8
 ISBN 978-0-87353-670-7   Stock No. 13798

Geometry for Teaching Mathematics in Grades 6–8
 ISBN 978-0-87353-691-2   Stock No. 14122

Functions for Teaching Mathematics in Grades 9–12
 ISBN 978-0-87353-623-3   Stock No. 13483

Geometry for Teaching Mathematics in Grades 9–12
 ISBN 978-0-87353-692-9   Stock No. 14123

Mathematical Reasoning for Teaching Mathematics in Prekindergarten–Grade 8
 ISBN 978-0-87353-666-0   Stock No. 13794

Proof and Proving for Teaching Mathematics in Grades 9–12
 ISBN 978-0-87353-675-2   Stock No. 13803

Forthcoming:

Developing Essential Understanding of—

Geometry for Teaching Mathematics in Prekindergarten–Grade 2

Geometric Shapes and Solids for Teaching Mathematics in Grades 3–5

Statistics for Teaching Mathematics in Grades 6–8

Statistics for Teaching Mathematics in Grades 9–12

Visit www.nctm.org/catalog for details and ordering information.